Freeing the Feminine

Freeing the Feminine

Elspeth and
Gordon Strachan

Labarum Publications Ltd
Dunbar

Labarum Publications Ltd

The Abbey, Dunbar, East Lothian, EH42 1JP,
Scotland.

British Library Cataloguing in Publication Data

Strachan, Elspeth
  Freeing the Feminine.
  1. Women in Christianity
  2. Women—Social conditions
  i. Title   ii. Strachan, Gordon
  261.8'3442   HQ1394

ISBN 0 948095 03 2

Printed by McCorquodale (Scotland) Ltd.

Contents

Preface

This book began its life among the carrots and quiches
of the Netherbow wholefood restaurant in Edinburgh.
As we chopped up the organic parsnips for vegetable
stew, cleared the tables and washed the dishes, it
occurred to us that we were involved in a more
traditionally feminine sphere of life. What we were
doing was 'woman's work'; the vegetables we were
chopping had been gathered from the lap of 'mother'
earth; they had grown in 'virgin' soil and owed their
health and beauty to the beneficence of 'mother' nature,
with her warm sunshine and life-giving rains. The
feminine imagery was very striking.

We enjoyed this work, knowing it to be healing,
creative, economically sound and of crucial importance
in terms of health and wholeness, but the church
authorities who owned the Netherbow Arts Centre were
unimpressed. What we were doing seemed far too
menial to them to be worthy of serious attention. As an
ordained minister and a history graduate we should have
been using our brains to preach and teach, not our hands
to serve and cook! But for us the excitement of the
kitchen and of the Netherbow Arts Centre as a whole
was that it brought together head and heart, mind and
hand, soul and body, art and craft, and represented a
more feminine approach in what we saw as an over-
masculine church and society.

We came to the Netherbow in 1974, at a time when groups such as Christian Aid and Oxfam were pleading for more practical compassion to be shown towards those millions of people in our world who are starving. They urged us not just to give more money, but to recognise that all life on this planet is one, that we are inextricably connected with each other. How we live affects others, they said, and so we in the west must learn to live more simply that others might simply live. In response to this challenge we decided to put basic needs before luxuries and to make the kitchen and cottage garden, rather than the theatre and galleries, the heart of the Netherbow. Although we appreciated the arts as an essential part of life's harmony and creativeness, as well as a powerfully prophetic medium, it seemed to us that before any harmony could be real the first priority was to recognise and meet people's basic needs. This changed our whole perception of life and our attitude to lifestyle. It was for this reason that we could be found working away in the restaurant, serving simple, vegetarian food and helping to dig our tiny cottage garden to produce herbs, flowers and vegetables to grace our tables. It became increasingly clear to us that what was needed was a new understanding of the feminine and a release of the feminine qualities in ourselves, our church and in society.

Another dimension to our desire to free the feminine was our interest in ecology. We began to see that if all life is one, then we have a responsibility not just towards our poorer neighbours, but towards all of creation. Conservationists were telling us that 'mother' earth on whom we depend for our very survival is exhausted and polluted by our industrial expansion and greed. She is in a state of rape, they said, and unless something is done to respect her needs and renew her fertility, we will be in serious danger ourselves. We discovered in the bible that

God's answer to the land's need for rest and renewal was for every seventh year to be fallow. This sabbatical year was an intrinsic part of the rhythms of creation and a biblical conservation strategy for all of nature, including humanity. Although the church refused to grant the Netherbow itself a sabbatical, after six years there, we decided to leave and take one ourselves. In an attempt to recover a sense of the rhythms of life and our unity with, rather than domination of nature, we went into the country to read and write, and try our hand at gardening.

This book is one of the fruits of that sabbatical year. Together we discussed, read and wrote about many of the issues covered here. Elspeth felt particularly drawn to explore the meaning of the masculine/feminine balance and the connection between women and nature, feminism and ecology. Gordon was fired by the desire to study the Romantic Movement and the bible's attitude to nature. This book is the fusion of our ideas. It was researched and written by Elspeth and edited by Gordon. The whole process has been one of growth, discovery and sharing and we feel very privileged to have been given the opportunity to think, study and work together in the way we have. There are many people to thank.

First of all, Alison and Philip Newell who shared in the stimulation and fun of many literary week-ends together, listening with critical attention to the first reading of our manuscripts; also Joanna Anderson for introducing Elspeth to many of the women's issues in the book and inspiring her to do her own study. Monica Furlong read the first draft and we are very grateful for her criticism and advice. It is not her fault that we didn't follow all of it! Sandy Burwell typed the initial draft and her enthusiasm was a tremendous encouragement.

We are very appreciative of John Gibson who kindly

read and commented on the manuscript, warning us of possible pitfalls, and David Armstrong who shared with us his vision of the New Age and gave very helpful and detailed criticism. Elspeth is particularly grateful for the unflagging support and stimulating cross-current of ideas from Clare Macrae, and for the loving determination with which Susan Cammack typed the second draft. She also wants to thank *Women Sharing* for showing that the way of the feminine does work.

Maryel Gardyne has been so much part of our lives and on-going discussion that it is almost impossible adequately to thank her. We would be much the poorer without her stimulation and vision. We are immensely grateful to those private people and trusts that have supported us financially since we started writing. Without their generosity our project would not have been possible. Our friends and families have been extremely tolerant of our necessary unsociability as we have wrestled with our ideas, and we thank them for their patient understanding and interest.

Finally we would like to thank our publisher, Clive Rawlins for his helpful and constructive criticism, and Rosemary Goring for creatively and tactfully pulling a jagged manuscript into shape.

Elspeth and Gordon Strachan
Edinburgh, September 1984.

Chapter One

The problem

In the aftermath of the first world war and long before the second, Sigmund Freud concluded an essay entitled *Civilization and its Discontents* with a question which he called 'the fateful question of the human species'— whether the human instincts of aggression, self-destruction and mastery of nature would so dominate our civilisation that life as we know it would cease to exist. 'Men have brought their powers of subduing the forces of nature to such a pitch' he wrote, 'that by using them they could now very easily exterminate one another to the last man. They know this—hence arises a great part of their current unrest, their dejection, their mood of apprehension.'[1] He foresaw a grim battle between the 'heavenly powers' of love and death over the fate of the human race, but could not predict the outcome.

Freud's question was posed in 1930. The full extent of the human drive to control and exploit nature was revealed in 1945 when the cataclysmic power of the atom was harnessed and made into the nuclear bomb. On August 6, at 8.16 am, this 'basic power of the universe' as President Truman described it, was unleashed over Hiroshima. The horrors of devastation to body, mind and spirit, the natural environment, human habitation and culture that resulted were beyond comprehension and out of all proportion to any previous human

1

experience. The technocrats who devised the bomb had become purveyors of death, mass destroyers of mankind. Freud's fateful question was being answered.

Despite the horrific effects of the splitting of the atom actually unleashed on hundreds of thousands of Japanese, our world today contains over a million times the destructive power of the Hiroshima bomb—enough to reduce the planet to 'a republic of insects and grass'.[2] If, as Freud feared, men and women were being made restless, anxious and unhappy by their unbridled mastery over nature as early as 1930, can we conceive the psychological effect that our modern potential for immediate global annihilation is producing when thoroughly weighed? All-out nuclear war is described as 'unthinkable', but too few of us really do consider the implications of the nuclear arms race. The terror and sheer bewilderment that such an all-embracing threat inevitably creates is still repressed by most people, shelved, unacknowledged and unvoiced. This repression is highly dangerous; it is one of the more sinister aspects of our nuclear age. As Jonathan Schell warns in his profoundly disturbing book *The Fate of the Earth*, it is our refusal to look at the practical realities of nuclear war that will bring us to the brink of it:

> At present, most of us do nothing. We look away. We remain calm. We are silent. We take refuge in the hope that the holocaust won't happen, and turn back to our individual concerns. We deny the truth that is all around us. Indifferent to the future of our kind, we grow indifferent to one another. We drift apart. We grow cold. We drowse our way toward the end of the world.[3]

While we drowse our way to the end of the world, barricading ourselves against our unrest, dejection and apprehension with increasingly sophisticated weapons of self-destruction, our death-in-life paralysis has become in itself a most lethal weapon, killing millions. The world's annual military bill amounts to hundreds of billions of dollars, yet something over thirty thousand people die *every day* from lack of that most basic human commodity—food. A fraction of even one day's military expenditure would help eradicate world hunger for ever, but our governments have neither the compassion nor the foresight to take this initiative. Despite the perceptive and urgent analysis of world problems by groups such as the Brandt Commission, we in the wealthy 'North' prefer to ignore the acute suffering of our neighbours of the 'South', believing that to do so will make our own survival more certain. This is tragically unrealistic, as the Brandt report shows.[4] For half the world to be dying of starvation while the other half spends millions on slimming diets and bombs is not only morally outrageous, it is economic suicide. As *North-South: a programme for survival* says,

> To diminish the distance between 'rich' and 'poor' nations, to do away with discrimination, to approach equality of opportunities step by step, is not only a matter of striving for justice, which in itself would be important. It is also sound self-interest, not only for the poor and very poor nations but for the better-off as well.[5]

Brandt calls for 'strong mutual interests in co-operation *and* . . . compassion'[6] and warns that without a new respect for qualities such as these our world will not survive.

What is wrong with our society that we have so little respect for care and compassion? We subdue the forces of nature, harnessing them for deadly purposes like the nuclear bomb; we repress our own natures, denying the dread caused in us by such a misuse of our creative

3

powers, and we stand idly by and watch millions of our fellow men, women and children wither and die, through our indifference and greed. We are cold, aggressive, detached and unfeeling, apparently caring neither for our true selves nor for others.

The qualities we seem to have lost, which are so much needed today, are those associated with the feminine pole of human experience: qualities such as care, co-operation, compassion, self-giving, nurturing and a sense of the continuity and oneness of life. Although traditionally associated with women, these attributes can of course be found in both women and men.

Over the years both women and the feminine side of human nature have been deemed inferior, of secondary importance and irrelevant if not troublesome to the serious business of running the world. By following the masculine way so exclusively, we have brought ourselves to the brink of self-destruction. Despite the rise of feminism and the success of a few notable women politicians, it is quite clear that masculine rather than feminine qualities are the ones valued in our leaders. This imbalance means that our world is ruled by impulses such as self-assertion, aggression, fierce independence, competition, ambition and 'logical' objectivity in a way that is now potentially lethal. We are taught to repress the feminine in ourselves, that side which relates to our emotions, intuitions and instincts. But such a repression creates disturbing personality problems which are becoming increasingly widespread, problems identical to the ones described by Jonathan Schell. Repression of the more feminine side of ourselves is a symptom of the psychological disorder called the schizoid condition. This is a condition which seems to permeate society today and it must be dealt with or it will lead us to our death.

In his book *Human Aggression* Anthony Storr

4

describes the schizoid person as cold, aloof, superior and detached with the potential for erupting into irrational violence.[7] Rollo May defines schizoid as 'out of touch; avoiding close relationships; the inability to feel'.[8] The word comes from the Greek *schizein* meaning to split, and although it has the same root as 'schizophrenic' it does not have the same meaning. Schizophrenia is a form of mental disorder whereas schizoid problems are common among perfectly 'normal' people. As Frank Lake points out in his analysis of schizoid personality reactions,

> . . . the learned professions contain many persons of the highest technical competence whose 'normality' in their jobs is unquestioned, who nevertheless react, as I do myself, under stress of commitment to certain kinds of emotional situation, in a deeply schizoid manner.[9]

The schizoid condition is very common but highly complex and difficult to analyse. It involves the cutting off or separation of the person from his or her feelings; the rejection of many physical and emotional needs and the sense of a split mind and body. In the individual it is a lack of love or inadequate loving patterns during the early months and first year of infancy which create this disorder. Separation at birth, neglect, abuse and alienation from the mother can cause unbearable pain to a young child for whom its mother is all-important. In the early stages a child has no sense of identity separate from the mother and is totally dependent on her. If she seems to reject her child, this breaks that essential bond. The child feels unloved, unlovable and forever wary of close emotional attachment. Although longed for and desperately needed, love comes to be seen only as a source of pain and disappointment, so defensive barriers are built up to protect the frightened child from further hurt. The mother herself is feared and rejected: no longer the source of comfort and nourishment, she is seen as the wicked witch who threatens to ensnare and devour.

By adulthood, these painful early experiences can result in making the individual seem cold, aloof and withdrawn, unable to relate deeply to others and afraid of expressing either physical or emotional warmth. There is at the same time a great desire for closeness, and a terror of it. Many schizoid sufferers escape into intellectual and spiritual abstractions becoming, for instance, dry academics, over-intellectual theologians, self-righteous spiritual leaders, or icily efficient businessmen and women. As personal contact and emotional needs cause deep anguish, ways of existing are sought which avoid the danger of being hurt. The wounded child is still there, however, and the early repression of feelings can be so deep and agonising that in later life the pressure may become intolerable and a sudden outburst results, often uncontrolled and violent.

In his book *Love and Will* Rollo May writes of the alarmingly high number of people coming for counselling for schizoid problems. He believes these problems to be in some way prophetic of our age—an indication of the unacknowledged inner dynamic of the society in which we live. 'Our patients are the ones who express and live out the subconscious and unconscious tendencies in the culture,' he writes.[10] He agrees with Anthony Storr's analysis as far as it goes, but argues that the lack of love, the disregard or rejection in infancy which causes the schizoid reaction is not merely the fault of the parents. Such parents are themselves victims of our modern society which offers few patterns of care, love and intimacy to follow:

> . . . I am contending that the schizoid condition is a general tendency in our transitional age, and that

6

the 'helplessness and disregard' in infancy to which Storr refers comes not just from parents but from almost every aspect of our culture. The parents are themselves unwitting expressions of their culture. The schizoid man is the natural product of the technological man.[11]

One area in which parents have been distressingly led astray by scientists and technology is in the nursing of small babies. Much in society teaches us to distrust our feelings, subdue our emotions and bring reason rather than intuition into play. The Truby King method of child-care, widely accepted and practised over fifty years ago, though now discredited, crystalised this teaching and applied it to the care of the new-born. According to King, from the moment of birth babies had to be fed by the clock rather than by their needs; they were not comforted when distressed unless it fitted the schedule and they were trained not to expect 'coddling'. Technological technique and scientific timetables replaced the mother's natural instincts, thereby severing the bond between mother and child. As Frank Lake observed,

> The time for which [the infants] could, with safety to their precariously developing trust be left alone, was regulated, not by the mother's delicate and sensitive intuition as to the state of the relationship in the 'nursing couple', but by prescription of the doctor or maternity nurses.[12]

He goes on to comment that

> The seeds of a profound distrust in the mother, the woman and 'god', as despising love needs and the hunger for sight or touch were sown in deep furrows, scored out across a once fair land. The harvest of emotionally impoverished . . . weedy personalities is being reaped.[13]

The tragedy is that such problems are perpetuated by children who have been brought up this way. Having had an inadequate example themselves of a loving, demonstrative relationship they often feel unable to show love to their own children. They cannot 'play it by ear', they cannot trust their feelings and instincts because their own condition does not allow it. Today, of course, child rearing is much more enlightened, but in the past those who followed the textbooks had this sort of advice given about the treatment of children:

> Never hug and kiss them. Never let them sit in your lap. If you must, kiss them once on the forehead when they say goodnight. Shake hands with them in the morning. Give them a pat on the head if they have made an extremely good job of a difficult task.[14]

This was written in 1928. It may be no coincidence that a society capable of producing such a manual went on to devise the nuclear bomb—a split atom for a split culture.

Rollo May suggests that the schizoid person is the natural product of our technological age. Technology has a tendency to depersonalise, to value size, speed and efficiency at the expense of community, organic growth and human contact. In those areas where the growth of technology is out of hand, such as in the world's major cities, personality problems are rife: depression, suicide and irrational violence are regular occurrences, and there is widespread apathy, listlessness, despair and vandalism. Apathy and violence seem to go hand in hand for, as Rollo May observed,

> The human being cannot live in a condition of emptiness for very long: if he is not growing *toward* something, he does not merely stagnate; the pent-

8

up potentialities turn into morbidity and despair, and eventually into destructive activities.[15]

In the summer of 1981 Britain experienced an outburst of unprecedented violence on the streets of some of her larger cities. The people who took part in the riots all expressed a profound and overwhelming sense of frustration and powerlessness. They came from decaying inner cities, crumbling relics of a past age where the centre of town was a thriving community. These areas are now ghettos and the young people who live there have felt very bitter about the way they are treated by the rest of society. Frequently they have no jobs, no social clubs, no decent housing, no respect outside their own group and no future. They feel alienated and rejected.

A similar sense of disorientation is felt by many urban dwellers, especially those who live in the large, inner city areas. Cities such as London, Manchester, Glasgow and Liverpool have particularly bad problems as a result of their size and overcrowding. It is significant that the police have been blamed for the tension and sense of alienation felt especially by minority communities, and a sign of our times that they no longer feel safe enough to go 'on the beat'. The friendly presence of the 'bobby' has been replaced by military-style tactics: patrol squads, radio communications and other technological tools. Debates over the need for community policing have reflected the cause-and-effect relationship between growth in technology and deep social problems.

The young people who exploded in the summer riots were expressing the more violent end-result of a mood of purposelessness that seems to permeate society. With unemployment high, many people with few inner resources to draw upon, give in to despair. According to May, this mood can be traced back to the radically transitional nature of our age where technology, efficiency, size and speed dominate over traditional patterns of community, co-operation and organic growth. As he comments,

> . . . ours is an era of radical transition. The old myths and symbols by which we oriented ourselves are gone, anxiety is rampant; we cling to each other and try to persuade ourselves that what we feel is love; we do not will because we are afraid that if we choose one thing or one person we'll lose the other, and we are too insecure to take that chance. . . . The individual is forced to turn inward; he becomes obsessed with the new problem of identity, namely, Even-if-I-know-who-I-am, I-have-no-significance. I am unable to influence others. The next step is apathy. And the step following that is violence. For no human being can stand the perpetually numbing experience of his own powerlessness.[16]

The 60s and 70s were dubbed the 'Me' decades because so many people were spending time trying to sort themselves out and discover who they really were. Today, traditional patterns are being consistently broken down, and the fear of commitment is a theme running through many relationships, encouraging isolation and self-absorption. Of course, great numbers of people are active in militating for a better lifestyle, more satisfying jobs, a secure future, and protest groups demanding the end to nuclear proliferation are gaining more and more support. However, these people remain on the fringe of society and the 'silent majority' stays at home, reading of increasingly regular incidences of muggings, rape, armed assault, terrorist activities and political assassination. Our world is indeed schizoid.

The findings of Rollo May regarding the effects of our new technological age have been confirmed by many psychologists and social scientists in different ways. Perhaps the most famous was F A Barnett's comparison between the behaviour of overcrowded rats and that of overcrowded people. Among the rats there was fierce and violent competition between the males, sudden death without visible cause, sexual deviance, neglect of and attack on the young. In vast overcrowded human conglomerates, the regular occurrences of violent street crimes, gang warfare, stress diseases, collapse of the family unit, sexual permissiveness and baby- and wife-battering have mirrored the distressed behaviour of the caged rats.[17]

It would be facile to imply that this is everyone's experience of the city. It can offer great security, a sense of community, stimulation and glamour, as well as ease and luxury of lifestyle. For many it provides the necessity of employment and future security. Nevertheless, there is disturbing evidence of a psychological imbalance resulting from the growth of city-life, at the expense of life in the country. Elaine Morgan, in her provocative book on urban decline laments the neglect of the countryside and the polarisation between urban and rural life. Quoting the impartial research of social scientists such as Louis Wirth, she describes the predominant characteristics of city dwellers:

> . . . as compared with folk communities, the city people now moving into the human majority tend to be more rational, more sophisticated, more tolerant, more secular, more reserved and more interdependent. They are also more liable to judge by appearances, and to be ambitious, competitive and cash-oriented.

There are equally striking tendencies on the negative side, however, remarkably similar to the findings of Rollo May:

11

> . . . . They are more predatory, more neurotic, more criminal, more likely to develop schizoid personalities and to conduct only fragmented relationships, and to suffer from that peculiarly urban malaise known as 'anomie'—a condition of apathy and hopeless disorientation caused by the breakdown of familiar and universally recognised rules of conduct.[18]

Dismay at the problems caused by the growth of large cities is not a modern phenomenon, despite the fact that they have now reached an unprecedented size. William Cobbett remarked that two hundred years before his time the size of London had aroused people's passions, with the increase of buildings being seen as 'no better than a wen or excrescence upon the body-politic'. 'What must we think' he asked, 'of those numberless streets and squares which have been added since!'[19] The industrial revolution had created havoc in London, Glasgow, Birmingham and many other cities throughout Britain. It was the age of the machine and the factory, and these—and therefore jobs—were not to be found in the villages, but in the towns. People of all ages left the countryside in vast numbers to find work in the factories, and houses had to be built to accommodate them. But these 'numberless streets and squares' brought with them a disorientation and anonymity which produced rootlessness and shrivelled the human spirit.

So great were the disturbances caused by these 'unnatural conglomerates' that in 1829 Sir Robert Peel decided that the country had outgrown her police institutions. It was to deal with the increased crime rate in the growing industrial cities that he set up his new police force and created the 'bobby'. These policemen were appointed as public servants, but encouraged to behave as ordinary private servants. Their friendly presence could do little, however, to assuage the overwhelming sense of isolation and disorientation experienced by those who had left their villages for the towns.

One of the major early records of the new city and its effects is William Wordsworth's seventh book of *The Prelude*. Although filled with 'wonder and obscure delight' at London's history and glories, he was nevertheless baffled by

> . . . how men lived
> Even next-door neighbours, as we say, yet still
> Strangers, nor knowing each the other's name.[20]

Literary critic Raymond Williams writes in *The Country and the City*, that Wordsworth was the first to express what has since become a dominant experience of the city. He felt a new sense of alienation, a strangeness, or loss of connection in the crowd of others which threatened his own sense of identity:

> O Friend! one feeling was there which belonged
> To this great city by exclusive right;
> How often, in the overflowing streets,
> Have I gone forwards with the crowd, and said
> Unto myself, 'The face of every one
> That passes by me is a mystery!'
> Thus have I looked, nor ceased to look, oppressed
> By thoughts of what and whither, when and how,
> Until the shapes before my eyes became
> A second-sight procession, such as glides
> Over still mountains, or appears in dreams.
> And all the ballast of familiar life,
> The present, and the past; hope, fear; all stays,
> All laws of acting, thinking, speaking man
> Went from me, neither knowing me, nor known.[21]

This is the 'anomie' which Elaine Morgan described—a sense of alienation and rejection which was perhaps first felt by those who had left the country to seek their fortunes in the new industrial cities. It created a deep split between the ways of nature and the new ways of men.

It was not only Wordsworth, however, who saw the evils of the city so clearly. Artists and writers of the time expressed the same tension between town and country. Frederick Engels for instance saw that the 'very turmoil of streets has something repulsive, something against which all human nature rebels'. Writing in 1844, he complained that the 'hundreds of thousands of all classes and all ranks . . . crowd by one another . . . and their only agreement is the tacit one, that each keep to his own side of the pavement, so as not to delay the opposing streams of the crowd, while it occurs to no man to honour another with so much as a glance'.[22] Engels accepted that selfishness and self-centredness are very much the condition of man, but was convinced that the 'brutal indifference, the unfeeling isolation of each in his private interest becomes the more repellent and offensive, the more these individuals are crowded together, within a limited space . . . it is nowhere so shamelessly barefaced, so self-conscious as just here in the crowding of the great city'. For Wordsworth it was nature which provided a true community and a real society. He felt acutely the contrast between the isolation of the city and the warmth of nature.

Wordsworth saw the hand and spirit of God in creation with a clarity and profundity that is intensely moving. He looked to nature as his highest guide, and was

> . . . well pleased to recognise
> In nature and the language of the sense

14

The anchor of my purest thoughts, the nurse,
The guide, the guardian of my heart, and soul
Of all my moral being.[23]

There were others, however, who saw the countryside
in a very different light. 'Nature averse to crime?' wrote
Swinburne paraphrasing the Marquis de Sade, 'I tell you
that nature lives and breathes by it; hungers at all her
pores for bloodshed; yearns with all her heart for the
furtherance of cruelty.'[24] These two diametrically
opposed views reflected the schizoid confusion of the
eighteenth and nineteenth centuries regarding that great
archetypal mother—nature. On the one hand she was
guide, guardian, nurse and messenger of God; on the
other she was cruel, vicious, bloodthirsty and ungovern-
able. Those who, like de Sade, saw nature as a cruel
goddess, red in tooth and claw, hostile to man,
threatening life and morals, rejoiced in the success of
industry in harnessing her power, and bending her to the
service of man. The prospect of her gaping wounds,
spitting fire at coal-pits and belching smoke in the
factories must have filled them with delight, and the ease
with which they came to straddle her rivers and plains
and dissect her mysteries must have reassured them that
she could in time be subdued and conquered.

The romantics were dismissed by many in their own
time as sentimental, womanish and self-indulgent;
worshipping a pagan goddess of nature and wallowing in
a cult of sensibility. But there is a sense in which they
were the fore-runners of today's ecologists. Like the
romantics, ecologists deplore the havoc caused to nature
by the world's ever-advancing industrialisation. But
equally like the romantics, many are dismissed as
idealistic, sentimental and self-indulgent. Their warnings are ignored and their cries for conservation often
ridiculed by government and vested interests. In-

creasingly over the past hundred years, those who have attempted to defend and protect nature have been over-ridden by those who desire to see her subdued and exploited. This conflict which began in earnest in the nineteenth century is one of the major causes of today's urban malaise.

In Wordsworth's and Engel's day the industrial city rarely reached a million inhabitants, although there was a staggering rise in them in contrast to previous centuries. Plato considered the ideal size of a city to be around thirty thousand inhabitants, as did Leonardo da Vinci. It would appear that the number of inhabitants in most medieval towns on the continent remained fairly steady over hundreds of years, between twenty-five and thirty-five thousand. The shock of the new cities of the industrial revolution was enormous; the shock of the monstrous growth of cities such as London, Tokyo and New York cannot be calculated. In the USA, sociologists no longer talk of the city, or even the metropolis, but find themselves discussing the social unrest of the 'megalopolis'. They divide the USA into three vast 'megalopolitan' areas of sixty million inhabitants each—a very far cry from Plato's republic of thirty thousand.

One of the most celebrated critics of our modern obsession with size was E F Schumacher. His highly acclaimed book *Small is Beautiful* is subtitled *A Study of Economics as if People Mattered* and its outstanding popularity reflects the need—frequently unvoiced—that many people feel for a more moderate and humane application of the fruits of technology. Schumacher was not against technology itself, far from it, but he believed it should be used in a way which was appropriate to the needs of the people. He had seen too much damage done to lives and environment by the crude introduction of inappropriate tools. According to him, man dominated by technology acts like a foreign body in the subtle

16

system of nature, and he saw numerous signs of rejection. His chief criticism was of our failure to recognise the need for moderation; he called for a balance between natural growth and our own apparently overwhelming desire to expand:

> Nature always, so to speak, knows where and when to stop. Greater even than the mystery of natural growth is the mystery of the natural cessation of growth. There is measure in all natural things—in their size, speed or violence. As a result, the system of nature, of which man is a part, tends to be self-balancing, self-adjusting, self-cleansing. Not so with technology, or perhaps I should say: not so with man dominated by technology and specialization.[25]

Writing forty years after Freud, Schumacher perceived the same unhappiness, unrest and anxiety caused by the human drive to subdue the forces of nature and 'prove' our superiority. He believed, like Freud, that our battle with nature could end with the destruction of ourselves. On the personal and medical level, the dethroning of the 'mother instincts' in favour of technological method and scientific 'objectivity' has caused a great deal of distress, and helped create disturbing personality disorders. But on the global level our dethroning of Mother Nature and our rejection of her organic wisdom, in favour of mechanistic industrialised expansion, is causing a scale of crisis which threatens not only our stability but our very survival. We appear to be doing our utmost not just to control and master nature, but to destroy her. Every day our ears are assailed with news of the latest catastrophe to our planet because of our uncontrolled determination to expand and industrialise. The trees of the West German Black Forest, for instance, are being eaten away by the pernicious effects of acid rain, as is the fish-life in the rivers and lakes of Northern Europe and Canada. Acid rain is fast becoming one of the most serious pollution problems of industrial countries. It is a direct result of the ever-growing quantities of industrial waste from fossil-fuels that are being belched into the sky from high stack chimneys, mixing with the weather systems and falling as sulphuric acid. It is the sheer size of this industrial build-up that creates the scale of the problem.

Even more serious than this destruction of trees and lakes is the accelerating annihilation of the world's vital rain forests. So important are they for replenishing and recycling the earth's atmosphere that they have been called the earth's lungs, yet they are being destroyed at the rate of fifty acres a minute, as a result of greed and mismanagement. Vital cropland is also being eroded through exhaustion and over-exploitation. It would appear that at current rates an area twice the size of Canada will have become desert by the year 2000 if nothing is done.[26] Many species of plant and animal wildlife also face extinction because of our disregard for their worth. One species actually dies out every ten minutes, some of them not even having been identified before they go. In 1980, the World Conservation Strategy launched a report on the state of the earth's natural resources. It made sombre reading. We are wreaking havoc on animal and plant wildlife, on oceans, atmosphere, rivers and rain-forest, and endangering our own lives in the process. Essential food and medical supplies are bound up in the nature we ignore so readily. As Robert Allen observed in his book *How to Save the World*,

> Earth is the only place we know of in the universe that can support human life. Yet human activities

18

are progressively making the planet less fit to live on. . . . Everywhere fertile soil is either being built on or flushed into the sea; otherwise renewable resources are exploited beyond recovery, and pollutants are thrown like wrenches into the machinery of climate. As a result, the planet's capacity to support people is irreversibly reduced at the very time when rising human numbers and consumption are making increasingly heavy demands upon it.[27]

There is a pyramid of destructive activities against nature, at the top of which sits our arsenal of nuclear bombs, primed to reduce the whole thing to something less than rubble.

We have bastioned ourselves against nature in concrete high-rise flats; invented ways of by-passing her rhythms through chemicals and drugs; processed, coloured and 'improved' her harvest of food. As far as possible, it would seem, we distance ourselves from anything natural, and warmly embrace the man-made. Those who cry for a more balanced, respectful treatment of nature are reminded that she is 'red in tooth and claw', unpredictable and cataclysmic in the violence of her earthquakes, volcanic eruptions, droughts and floods. Attitudes such as these have led to the ecological crisis that faces us today. Too many people still believe that our survival depends on how well we protect ourselves against nature, rather than how well we protect her against *us*.

Warnings have been issued, however, and not only in the past few years. As long ago as 1854, the American Indian Chief Seattle, delivered a powerful message to President Franklin Pierce, who wanted to buy his lands, warning him that he and his people must not abuse the earth, the sky and beasts, but love them as members of their own families:

19

> Teach your children what we have taught our children: that the earth is our mother. Whatever befalls the earth befalls the sons of the earth. If men spit upon the ground, they spit upon themselves. . . . Continue to contaminate your bed and you will one night suffocate in your own waste.

Those words of Chief Seattle have a prophetic and chilling ring to them today, as talks continue over the consequences of our pollution of the entire planet, and as governments become increasingly worried.

For the North American Indians, the earth was their mother. She nourished them, protected them, offered her wisdom to them and received them back into her body when they died. For this they gave her great respect, reverence and love, some refusing even to plough her soil because it was her body:

> You ask me to plow the ground. Shall I take a knife and tear my mother's breast? Then when I die she will not take me to her bosom to rest.

> You ask me to dig for stone. Shall I dig under her skin for her bones? Then when I die I cannot enter her body to be born again.

> You ask me to cut grass and make hay and sell it and be rich like white men. But how dare I cut off my mother's hair?[28]

The white man's treatment of nature was simply beyond their comprehension. As Chief Seattle so rightly observed,

> He treats his mother, the earth, and his brother the sky as things to be bought, plundered, sold like sheep or bright beads. His appetite will devour the earth and leave behind only a desert.

The American Indians had a much more mature, loving concern for the mother earth, just as mature and healthy adults love and respect their natural mother. In comparison, western men and women act as schizoid infants, unfeeling towards her constraints, rejecting her nourishment, warmth and co-operation, building up continuously stronger barriers against her.

We are faced with possible extinction as a direct consequence of our acts of earth-violation. Coldly aloof, superior and detached, we have moved against our soils, our forests, our oceans and our very air itself in acts of fearful destruction. Our schizoid world has chosen the 'cleverness' of technological technique rather than the wisdom of nature. But just as the child, however schizoid, must receive care and nourishment from its mother if it is to survive, despite its rejection of her, so our schizoid culture depends utterly on the rhythms, harvests and stability of nature, despite our alienation from her. If we are engaged in a battle against nature, then it is we who will inevitably lose. We cannot survive without her, as the poet Ted Hughes reminds us in his *Revenge Fable:*

There was a person
Could not get rid of his mother
As if he were her topmost twig.
So he pounded and hacked at her
With number and equations and laws
Which he invented and called truth.
He investigated, incriminated
And penalized her . . . .
Forbidding, screaming and condemning,
Going at her with a knife,
Obliterating her with disgusts
Bulldozers and detergents

21

> Requisitions and central heating
> Rifles and whisky and bored sleep.
>
> With all her babes in her arms, in ghostly weepings,
> She died.
>
> His head fell off like a leaf.

For Ted Hughes, nature was a passive, subservient mother figure who died quietly and in deep agony. Ecologist Kit Pedler had a very different picture of her: he saw nature as a raging revolutionary, furious at the damage being done and fully determined to put it right—with or without our help. Pedler was highly critical of what he called the 'reductionist technologist toymakers'—those who use their intelligence and expertise to dissect nature's mysteries and create clever new technological tools, regardless of their usefulness or potential harm. They see the whole of life as something that can be fully understood simply by analysing its parts. They 'murder to dissect' and 'assert that there are no values in the universe; no beauty, no rhythm and no regard, care or love, just systems for analysis and exploitation'.[29] Pedler makes a plea for the holistic view which sees life as a whole, much more than the sum of its parts:

> Stretching from man to the worm, from the fishes of the abyss to the yoghurt bacterium, and from the moulds of decay to the birds riding the sky, I hold that there is but one single interwoven web of life and that our own kind was, until recently, an integral part of this single magnificent entity.[30]

Pedler calls this entity, this life-force, Gaia. 'I use the name Gaia,' he explains, 'not to propose a human feminine goddess, but to encompass the idea that the entire living pelt of our planet, its thin green rind of life, is actually one single life-form with senses, intelligence and the power to act.'[31] Nevertheless, Gaia was the name of a goddess and this is highly significant. She is the Greek Earth Mother and mother of the gods.

In identifying the spirit of nature with a goddess Pedler was following an ancient tradition. The figure of the goddess of the earth can be found all over the world and many myths have been built up around her. But, as Pedler points out, they all share the idea that the earth is not a dead body. As we have seen, the American Indians called the earth 'mother', but there are similar indigenous traditions in Europe and elsewhere.

Many of us have forgotten the ancient stories about Mother Earth and the Great Goddess, but they are of vital importance in understanding ourselves, our culture and our inherited attitudes to the earth, women and the feminine aspects of life. The Great Mother is an archetypal figure who lives in what Jung called the 'collective unconscious' of all humanity—that part of our psyche which retains the impressions gathered in the earliest experiences of humankind. As Jung said,

> Today . . . we talk of 'matter'. We describe its physical properties. We conduct laboratory experiments to demonstrate some of its aspects. But the word 'matter' remains a dry, inhuman, and purely intellectual concept, without any psychic significance for us. How different was the former image of matter—the Great Mother—that could encompass and express the profound emotional meaning of Mother Earth.[32]

We have lost touch with the emotional energy in the image of the Great Mother, and with the holistic view of life which saw no division between spirit and matter or heaven and earth.

Many ecologists today assume that to encourage us to call earth 'mother' will provoke a radically respectful response, but they forget that modern society is schizoid and the mother-figure, whether nature, the woman or the goddess, is deeply suspect. Society unquestionably has a paradoxical attitude to the traditionally feminine aspects of life. On the one hand there is a tacit and pernicious assumption that the feminine is inferior to the masculine, that women are weak, passive and exploitable, that nature is only there to be subdued. But on the other hand there is the hint of ancient and deeply disturbing powers which, like the angry mother, the wicked witch or cataclysms of nature, threaten to overwhelm and destroy. Nature is the mother whom our schizoid anxieties force us to reject, but we are paying the price—jeopardising our humanity and our future. In the words of Jung,

> As scientific understanding has grown, so our world has become dehumanised. Man feels himself isolated in the cosmos, because he is no longer involved in nature, and has lost his emotional 'unconscious identity' with natural phenomena. These have slowly lost their symbolic implications. Thunder is no longer the voice of an angry god, nor is lightning his avenging missile. No river contains a spirit, no tree is the life principle of a man, no snake the embodiment of wisdom. . . . His contact with nature has gone, and with it has gone the profound emotional energy that this symbolic connection supplied.[33]

According to the teaching of many Christian churches such an attitude is nothing more than mere pantheism, reflecting a pre-Christian, pagan view of nature, which worships creation itself rather than the creator. But then much of the church's teaching is also schizoid in its attitude to the feminine side of life, including nature. The evidence of the bible shows that nature is the messenger, the voice, the avenger and the glory of her Creator-God who dwells in the heavens and on earth,

> Who makest the clouds thy chariots,
> Who ridest on the wings of the wind,
> Who makest the winds thy messengers,
> fire and flame thy ministers.
>
> (Ps. 104:3, 4)

Schizoid churches have neglected this aspect of biblical truth by escaping into false mental and ecclesiastical abstractions. They have repressed the feminine in their midst. The example and teaching of Jesus Christ showed a better way. As God made man, uniting heaven and earth, spirit and matter in his very being, he is the redeemer and creator our schizoid world so desperately needs. Yet, as Lake laments, 'The redeemer the schizoid sufferer needs is precisely the redeemer the schizoid intellectual theologian has compulsively striven to abolish'.[34] Too often our churches are but a mirror of society, reflecting some of its worst attitudes. Our reductionist society also has reductionist churches which seem to have little concept of the oneness of all creation, content to teach the disunity they practise by offering a dualism between spirit and matter, masculine and feminine, man and woman. Such divisions are deeply destructive.

If, as Rollo May believes, our schizoid sense of alienation, apathy and violence are all partly caused by our being out of touch with the truth behind the myths, symbols and traditional patterns which have made up our past, then we would do well to try to rediscover their meaning. It would be especially helpful to try to learn more about that powerful archetypal figure the Great Mother and her appearance in history. Our modern determination to subdue nature may be due to an unacknowledged fear of the destructive power of our own instinctual nature, or an irrational fear of the power of the ancient goddess. If we go back in time and look at some of the earlier myths and traditions on which society is based, we may be given a new perspective on our problem, which will enable us to begin to consider why the earth and her inhabitants have suffered such abuse at the hands of an essentially hostile human race. We may also begin to uncover the roots of society's deeply schizoid condition.

Chapter Two

In the beginning . . .

Before Heaven and Earth existed
There was something nebulous:
Silent, isolated,
Standing alone, changing not,
Eternally revolving without fail,
Worthy to be called Mother of All Things.
I do not know its name
And address it as Tao.
If forced to give it a name, I shall call it 'Great'.[1]

This beautiful Chinese poem, believed to have been written in the sixth century BC by the philosopher Lao-tse, expresses most eloquently a concept which has its roots in the world's earliest religious traditions, namely, that in the beginning of time there was a mysterious, transcendent, all-embracing Presence who was the potential source of life and therefore worthy to be called 'Mother'. The Taoist philosophy of Lao-tse was highly sophisticated and he was reluctant to give this great Presence a name, for that would limit it. Nevertheless he did consider it appropriate to call this being 'Mother of All Things' and 'Great'. Other religious traditions have been less reticent about naming this great maternal being, and her titles are myriad. They range from Queen of Heaven, Mother Earth and Tellus Mater, to Creatress of the Gods and Great Mother. Her worship was one of the earliest manifestations of religious belief and this was not as a mere fertility figure. Primarily she was identified with nature, but not exclusively. The following address, found in Apuleius's *The Golden Ass* gives some indication of her grandeur:

> I am Nature, the universal Mother, mistress of all the elements, primordial child of time, sovereign of all things spiritual, queen of the dead, queen also of the immortals, the single manifestation of all gods and goddesses that are. My nod governs the shining heights of Heaven, the wholesome sea breezes, the lamentable silences of the world below. Though I am worshipped in many aspects, known by countless names, and propitiated with all manner of different rites, yet the whole round earth venerates me.[2]

In terms of the history of the worship of the Mother Goddess, this testimony is relatively recent, yet its sentiments transcend time. Even today this great maternal deity is being worshipped with considerable devotion. For the Kagaba people of Colombia in South America, for instance, she is 'the only mother we possess':

> The mother of our songs, the mother of all our seed, bore us in the beginning of things and so she is the mother of all types of men, the mother of all nations. She is the mother of the thunder, the mother of the streams, the mother of trees and of all things . . . .
> She has no cult, and no prayers are really directed to her, but when the fields are sown and the priests chant their incantations the Kagaba say, "And then we think of the one and only mother of the growing things, of the mother of all things."[3]

Although this supreme being is associated with
maternal imagery, nevertheless in her capacity as creatress of the gods and of all heaven and earth, she was
understood to contain and transcend both feminine *and*
masculine characteristics. She was a great androgynous
deity who would not be limited by sex or gender. In the
previous chapter we heard of the Greek goddess Gaia.
She was the primeval Mother Earth from whose womb
Heaven (Uranos), the mountains, valleys, vegetation
and lesser gods and goddesses were born. She 'emerged
from Chaos and bore her son Uranos as she slept'.[4]
Implicit in the archetypal Great Mother was her capacity
to contain all life in its complexity within her cosmic
womb. She could therefore fertilise herself without need
of a male consort, and bring to maturity the embryo of
the world. This ability also gave her the paradoxical title
Virgin Mother.

The waters of the Virgin's magical womb were
analogous to the primeval waters that were believed to
exist in a state of chaos before creation began. In Genesis 1,
for example, the word for 'the deep' is *tehōm*, which is
related etymologically to Tiamat ('Ocean'), the Babylonian goddess of the primeval ocean. In the
Egyptian Coffin texts dating from 2250–1580 BC the
Egyptian High God describes himself as 'the spirit in the
Primeval Waters', the 'drowned one':

> I was (the spirit in?) the Primeval Waters,
> he who had no companion when my name came
>   into existence.
> The most ancient form in which I came into
>   existence was as a drowned one.
> I was (also) he who came into existence as a circle,
> he who was the dweller in his egg.[5]

The cosmic circle or egg is another recurrent image in
many world myths and also relates to the womb of the

Great Mother. Just as in the human womb the embryo lives in an unconscious state with no sense of identity or differentiation, so in many creation myths the embryo of the world is first pictured as an egg in which the yolk and white are undifferentiated. Heaven, earth, and all the opposites of life are contained within the shell, but in an unseparated state at first. The following eighth-century Japanese creation myth is a good example of this tradition:

> Of old, Heaven and Earth were not yet separated, and the In and Yo not yet divided. They formed a chaotic mass like an egg, which was of obscurely defined limits and contained germs. The purer and clearer part was thinly diffused and formed Heaven, while the heavier and grosser element settled down and became Earth. The finer element easily became a united body, but the consolidation of the heavy and gross element was accomplished with difficulty. Heaven was therefore formed first, and Earth established subsequently. Thereafter divine beings were produced between them.[6]

Although there is no named maternal presence in this picture, there is the implicit recognition of some great feminine impulse which originally produced the egg-concept. These, and many other stories of the Great Mother with her primeval womb and miraculous powers of creation have a lyrical beauty which is perhaps surprising to our modern minds, and in direct contrast to the popular picture of the mother goddess in the west today.

The very word 'goddess' seems to conjure up images of a pagan, orgiastic fertility figure of minimal importance in the pantheons of the deities and totally subservient to the supreme high gods. As a participant in the vegetation fertility rites, she is seen as wholly concerned with sexuality and prostitution. There is no doubt that in some of its manifestations throughout history, the religion of the goddess has been cruel, blood-thirsty and promiscuous. In some forms it has involved cultic marriages, human and animal sacrifices, self-castration and sacred prostitution. These cannot be ignored. Just as nature can be both kind and cruel, gentle and vicious, so the Great Mother who is said to give birth to nature can also be both life-giving and death-dealing. In her positive aspect she was the great creator, sustainer and protector of life, governing 'the shining heights of heaven'; in her negative role she was the devouring, ensnaring dealer of death, unfaithful wife, cruel mother and ruler of "the lamentable silences of the world below". Her dual character as both creator and destroyer is revealed in one Latin inscription to Astarte which reads:

> Diva Astarte, hominum deorumque via, vita, salus: rusus eadam quae est pernicies, mors, interitus (Divine Astarte, the power, the life, the health of men, and gods, and the opposite of this which is evil, death and destruction).[7]

When we are considering the religious rites surrounding the worship of the goddess, however, it is important to remember their antiquity, for they were being practised at a time when such things as human sacrifice and cultic prostitution were common. The goddess religion dates as far back as 5000 BC in organised form—long before bible times. We cannot judge the morality of early religions by modern standards. The vegetation cults of the goddess are most commonly dismissed as depraved and superstitious. Yet, according to the distinguished Assyriologist Stephen Langdon, this is too simplistic. While very aware of the dark, vicious side of the rites, he also discovered in his researches a very much more

31

elevated, spiritual aspect which has generally been ignored. Writing in 1914 about the Babylonian vegetation cult, involving Tammuz and Ishtar he said this:

> The mysteries of the death and resurrection of the youthful god, the weeping mother and her descent to the shades of Aralu, were probably represented in some material way, but the chants themselves have little reference to such things. They are both spiritual and thoroughly human, poetical and skilfully liturgical.[8]

Of the cult itself he said:

> The consciousness that human life is unstable, transient, and full of sorrow, gave rise to asceticism, fasting and the adoration of eternal life. The measure of development of such a cult is a sure test of the culture of a people, and measured by this test the Babylonian religion ranks high among the great culture religions of antiquity.[9]

This is a very different picture of the goddess religion from the one usually presented by teachers and textbooks, but Langdon is not alone in his analysis. More recently Professor John Bright, in his acclaimed *History of Israel,* warns against over-simplification. While highly critical of the fertility rites in the Canaanite religion, he also points out that it was not devoid of more elevated aspects such as social concern for others.[10]

That the great Mother Goddess was ruler of love, fertility and the family, none would deny; yet the hymns, laments and liturgies of the period indicate that she was much more than that. She was also venerated as a warrior, a ruler of battles, a hunter, a shepherdess, a law-giver, judge, healer, teacher and prophet, as well as maker of heaven and earth. Her many names and titles reflected her different roles. Some of her complexity is revealed in her address to Apuleius:

> The primeval Phrygians call me Pessinunctica, Mother of the gods; the Athenians, sprung from their own soil, call me Cecropian Artemis; for the islanders of Cyprus I am Paphian Aphrodite; for the archers of Crete I am Dictynna; for the triligual Sicilians, Stygian Proserpine; and for Eleusinians their ancient Mother of the Corn.[11]

She goes on to say that although others know her as Juno, Bellona of the Battles, or Hecate and Rhamnubia, it is the Ethiopians and especially the Egyptians who know her true name:

> . . . both races of Aethiopians, whose lands the morning sun first shines upon, and the Egyptians who excel in ancient learning and worship me with ceremonies proper to my godhead, call me by my true name, namely, Queen Isis.[12]

The Egyptian goddess Isis was one of the greatest syncretistic mother goddesses combining in herself the attributes of some of the most ancient and powerful female deities of surrounding countries. According to E O James, '. . . [Isis] unquestionably was the greatest and most beneficent female deity, personifying all that was most vital in motherhood.'[13] She came to be equated with the Magna Mater of western Asia, Greece and Rome, and in her attributes became indistinguishable from the Hebrew Astarte and the Babylonian Ishtar. Her name meant literally 'seat' or 'throne', and as James observed, '. . . since enthronement has long been an essential element in royal installation, "the throne which made the king" readily would become the Great Mother charged with the mysterious power of kingship.'[14]

In its later manifestations the religion of Isis became

highly spiritualised and ascetic, and the image of her seated on a throne with the god Osiris on her knee was actually adopted by later Christian artists to depict Mary and Christ. Rosemary Radford Ruether has pointed out:

> The religion of Isis, the Egyptian goddess, was one prototype of many of the ideas taken over in Christian teaching about Mary. Chastity typified her image and worship. Her priests were tonsured and celibate. Fasting, prayer, vigils, and moral renewal preceded the initiation of her devotees. She appeared as a beautiful figure who rose from the sea, crowned with a moon, wearing a dark mantle bordered with stars. On the basis of moral renewal of their lives, her devotees were promised prosperity in this life and assurance of life after death. She was above all wisdom, the companion of purified souls. When the religion of Isis was defeated by Christianity, much of her power and attraction lived on in the devotion to Mary.[15]

As we can see, the Great Mother Goddess was a highly complex and paradoxical figure, often androgynous and frequently with conflicting qualities. Although a female deity, she was not a purely 'feminine' figure. She was a complex representative of all human qualities, masculine and feminine. However, the single most important factor in her worship has been her maternity. Even her androgyny was part of this for, as James remarks, '. . . divine androgyny has been a recurrent phenomenon in the Goddess cult everywhere, reflecting the primeval cosmic unity from which all creation has been thought to have emerged.'[16] The reason for the primacy of maternity in the goddess worship lies in the prehistoric past.

Among the earliest archaeological finds relating to primitive religions has been a number of female figurines which we call 'Venuses'. These statuettes were of full-breasted women, either pregnant or with their maternal attributes clearly emphasised. They were discovered in central and western Europe and date back to between 25,000 and 30,000 BC. Although it is considered unlikely that at that early stage these figurines represented an actual deity, it is clear that they did represent the mysteries of womanhood and motherhood. It is very significant that these Venuses were found in hunting communities where agricultural and vegetation rites were not known. This would appear to rule out the possibility that they were simply animistic representations of a vegetation fertility cult. It is far more likely, as anthropologists have observed, that these statuettes were linked to the mysteries of the woman as mother.

It is the assumption of many anthropologists that in earliest times the role of men in the procreative act was not understood, as is the case in some primitive tribes even today.[17] If this was so, then women would naturally have been seen to possess some stupendously miraculous ability to produce and feed children. This power would be of crucial importance in societies where nourishment was a matter of life and death. This gave them a special *mana* or religious significance associating women with wisdom, mystery and magic. It was out of this understanding that the idea of the Virgin Mother developed—the Great Mother who was creatress of all life and who contained all that was necessary for the birth and sustenance of the human species inside her own womb. Since they were unaware of the physiological process of generation, the earliest people had no way of protecting the continuation of the human species, so the role of the mother in the family must have been of primary importance. At a time when survival was a question of braving hostile elements, when storms, floods, droughts, earthquakes and disease could bring immediate annihilation, and when the precariousness of finding food and shelter must have been a constant source of anxiety, it was the figure of the all-knowing, all-embracing mother to whom the early earth-dwellers turned for protection, aid and comfort.

This mother could not, of course, reign unchallenged forever. Eventually it must have occured to the men, and indeed the women, that the sexual process was more complex yet more predictable than they had realised. It seems probable that in general this realisation dawned around the time when communities were changing from hunters to stock-raisers and from gatherers to farmers. This led to new religious practices. E O James explains:

> As the great Mother became more clearly defined, and consciousness of the duality of male and female in procreation was recognised increasingly, from being Unmarried Mother personifying the divine principle in maternity she was associated with the young god as her son and consort. Then, while she remained the crucial figure, the goddess cult assumed a twofold aspect in the ancient seasonal drama in which both the partners in generation played their respective roles of creative energy, the one female and receptive, the other male and begettive. From Neolithic times onward, phallic emblems were increasingly prevalent, though maternal imagery was predominant in Western Asia, and the Eastern Mediterranean, where in the first instance the male god was subordinate to the goddess.[18]

As the dual roles in the act of procreation were recognised, the mother inevitably lost her monopoly of generative and spiritual power. She now needed a consort to produce life. As agricultural practices developed and increased in importance, so did vegetation fertility rites, for survival was still precarious and dependent both on finding rich soil and being assured of regular rains. The fecundity of a woman's womb, her intimate connections with the rhythms of her body through menstruation, child-birth and lactation, as well as her apparently passive role in receiving the male 'seed' made her an obvious symbol to early peoples of the fertility of the earth, the rhythms and cycles of the seasons and the passivity of the soil in receiving the seeds of vegetation. The man's apparent transcendence over the rhythms of his body while producing the life-giving semen led to the association between man and the transcendent sky or heavens which produced the fertilising rains. Thus there developed a sacred cult marriage in which the goddess became the earth-mother and her consort became sky-father. There were many exceptions to these transferences of earth-mother and sky-father, for instance, in Egypt where the sky deity was the goddess Nut and the earth was her brother Geb, but in general the earth came to be seen as feminine and the sky or heavens masculine. The sacred marriage of heaven and earth was an early manifestation of the recognition that both male and female, masculine and feminine forces were needed in the creation of all life.

As a sign of this new awareness, as James emphasises, phallic symbols became increasingly prominent from Neolithic times onward. It is significant that these symbols and the development of a sacred marriage rite began to appear during the Neolithic period—at a time when some degree of mastery of nature was being achieved in the form of farming and herding. The discovery of male sexual potency and the introduction of a sky-father paralleled the growing human ability to transcend the bondage of nature and move away from an-almost unconscious identification with her to a conscious determination to master her forces.

This process also led to the domination of women by men. When society knew only its mothers the question of parentage was simple—the connection was obvious, physical, natural and binding. Establishing the paternity of a child, however, was a very much more uncertain affair. It required not only logical reasoning and self-control, but also the curtailing of a woman's freedom in a wide range of social aspects. Her 'nature' had to be subdued and her relationships with other men restricted. She became in effect, the man's private property.[19] She became the stronger partner's 'garden', and her children his 'produce'. As we would expect, the masculine drive to control the instinctive powers of nature, in particular of women and of their representative Mother Goddess, is revealed in many of the earliest myths and legends.

One of the most famous epic struggles is that contained in the Babylonian account of creation the *Enuma Elish*. Written towards the end of the second millenium BC, it tells how Marduk, new champion of the gods, set about destroying Tiamat, goddess of the primeval ocean. In Mesopotamia the essence of ancient religious belief was that the universe should be ordered, that chaos was evil and that whatever was above in the heavens should also be reflected below on earth. The forces of chaos in Babylon were represented by the Great Goddess Tiamat. Marduk, a much younger god challenged her to single combat, because:

> Against Anshar, king of the gods, thou seekest evil;
> (Against) the gods, my father, thou hast confirmed thy wickedness.[20]

The great Tiamat was furious at this precocious young

upstart's audacity and in fury cried aloud, but she had met her match:

> Then joined issue Tiamat and Marduk, wisest of the
>   gods.
> They strove in single combat, locked in battle.
> The lord spread out his net to enfold her,
> The Evil Wind, which followed behind, he let loose
>   in her face.
> When Tiamat opened her mouth to consume him,
> He drove in the Evil Wind that she close not her
>   lips.
> As the fierce winds charged her belly,
> Her body was distended and her mouth was wide
>   open.
> He released the arrow, it tore her belly,
> It cut through her insides, splitting the heart.
> Having thus subdued her, he extinguished her life.
> He cast down her carcass to stand upon it.[21]

This was not merely a battle between a feeble young goddess and a great lord. The intense violence shown towards Tiamat is an indication of the threat she was felt to be. Marduk crushed her skull and severed her arteries, spreading her out across the heavens; making of her one half the heavens, of the other half the earth. His fathers were joyful and jubilant, but he was still watchful:

> Half of her he set up and ceiled it as sky,
> Pulled down the bar and posted guards.
> He bade them to allow not her waters to escape.[22]

This Babylonian creation myth was repeated once a year at the New Year festival as part of a ritual drama to reaffirm the power of order over chaos; it ended with the all-triumphant cry 'Marduk is King!'

Marduk protected the military supremacy of Babylon, the authority of the king on the political and social levels, and it was hoped that he would prevent natural disasters such as drought, disease and earthquake from overtaking the people. He became the chief god of Babylon, and he won the people's respect. His authority, however, depended on the prosperity and importance of his own city. Those sky-gods such as Anu, Enlil and Enki who were supreme deities avoided this problem by becoming totally transcendent and uninvolved in the ordinary lives of humanity. However, the price they paid for this was that although recognised to be the supreme heads of the pantheon of lesser gods and goddesses, they were often too distant and otiose to gain the affection of the people. They seemed much too far away in the transcendent heights of heaven and unconcerned about the daily cares of the mere mortals whom they ruled. Many of these celestial gods were eclipsed by younger, more virile sons, as was the case in Canaan where El was outshone by his son Baal. However, in Mesopotamia, and indeed throughout western Asia and the near east, even these younger sons could not compete with the continuing splendour of the Mother Goddess herself.

Although she had lost her independent status as sole creator of life and as Virgin Mother, although her monopoly had been challenged by the new race of male gods, and although the primeval goddesses such as Tiamat had been defeated, the goddess's ancient religion was still very strong and could not be rooted out. It continued to capture the hearts and minds of the people. In theory she may have been under the authority of the Supreme High Gods, but in practice it was she who ruled. As James said 'From India to the Mediterranean, in fact, she reigned supreme, often appearing as the unmarried goddess.'[23] Although unmarried, she was still a mother and this was perhaps her primary role, but it was not a subservient one. Langdon observed, 'Having cast off many concrete qualities which were personified into female consorts of local gods, she retains for herself the commanding position of a detached deity, mother of humanity, defender of her people.'[24]

The Mother Goddess's pride of place was due to her crucial role in the seasonal vegetation drama of the dying and rising god. In this drama the young god represented the vegetation which withered and died in the summer drought or autumn cold. As he died, the goddess became the lamenting mother, grief-stricken in her bereavement and determined to restore him to life. Said Langdon, 'In the service of this cult the figure of the father god *an* is a mere shadow to explain the existence of the mother and son.'[25] It was the Mother Goddess who embodied the source of life. So James points out:

> In the primeval and perennial struggle between the two opposed forces in the seasonal sequence, manifest in the creative powers of spring and the autumnal decline, dearth and death, the Goddess was always supreme because she was the source of life, and her male partner was only secondarily her spouse. In short, the creative powers were secondary, and dependent upon forces over which man had but a limited measure of control.[26]

As the maternal source of life, it was the goddess who sought the dying son in the underworld and brought him back to life, not any male god. This coincided with the blossoming of spring after the ravages of winter. There is no doubt who was the dominant figure in this rite. It was he, not she, who died as the vegetation faded, and it was because of her life-giving capacities that he was reborn. He bowed to her awe-inspiring power, becoming her submissive son, following her commands and dying as a symbol of the reproductive forces to be renewed as the seasons changed.

The great goddess of Babylonia, Ishtar, was one of the oldest and most powerful Mother Goddesses of all time. In organised form her worship dates back before 3000 BC.[27] Her son's name, Tammuz, meant 'faithful son' and her own title was Queen of Heaven. So widespread was her worship that the name Ishtar came to be a synonym for 'goddess' in the near east.[28] Like Isis she was a great syncretistic deity and had many symbols, including the serpent, the asherah or stylised pillar, and the lion. One of her temples was called Eanna, and was situated in Uruk, biblical Erech, which was very near Ur. It was here that many sacred rituals took place. Her son Tammuz had no temple of his own. His worship was entirely identified with his mother. Nineveh, that great city against which Jonah was forced to preach with such spectacular results, was also widely regarded for the worship of Ishtar.

Something of the grandeur of this Great Mother as mother of sorrows is revealed in an early liturgy in which she is described seeking her son in the under-world. On her way to hades she is accosted by the gatekeeper who discourages her from going further because he fears that she will meet the queen of hades and this is forbidden. But she is determined to go on:

> O Innini, go not; the queen of the great house
> Not should'st thou know; not shouldst thou enter.
> Not shalt thou press forward, not shalt thou know
>   . . .
> But the maiden went, to the darkness went.
> 'A queen am I' (she said); the maiden went, to the
>   darkness went
> To him seized away, her beloved not should she go,
>   into darkness go.
> In the place of desolation among the hungry ones
>   she should not sit.[29]

42

Innini-Ishtar was a great queen who would not be overawed by anyone, even the queen of hades. At considerable risk to her own life she eventually found Tammuz, her beloved son, and brought him back to life. The flowers blossomed, the leaves of the trees burst forth, the young animals leapt from their mother's wombs and the people were no longer hungry and lamenting.

Although Ishtar's role as Mater Dolorosa was central to her status, she also had many other attributes and her authority was unchallenged even among the gods. As Great Mother she was both giver of life *and* destroyer of it, both loving mother and terrible mother, both virgin and harlot. She was the patroness of sexual love and family life; she was also judge, prophet, healer and goddess of war. Her word, for the Babylonians at least, was supreme among the gods as the following extract from a 1600 BC hymn shows:

> Ishtar among the gods, extraordinary is her station
> Respected is her word; it is *supreme* over them.
> She is their queen; they continually cause her
>   demands to be executed.
> All of them bow down before her.
> They receive her light before her.
> Women and men indeed revere her.[30]

In another prayer of the first millenium BC, Ishtar is described in the most glowing and splendid terms. It is a prayer of lamentation in which her supplicant asks for his sins to be forgiven. He praises her ability to heal the sick and raise the dead as well as to rule battles and govern heaven and earth. He is clearly in distress and feels that his lady has turned her face from him, but he reminds her that he has remained true to her, 'I have paid heed to thee, my Lady; my attention has been

turned to thee.' The genuine love and devotion in this
prayer to valiant Ishtar is unmistakable:

> I pray to thee, O Lady of ladies, goddess of
> goddesses.
> O Ishtar, queen of all peoples, who guides mankind
> aright,
> O Irnini ever exalted, greatest of the Igigi,
> O most mighty of princesses, exalted is thy name.
> Thou art indeed the light of heaven and earth, O
> valiant daughter of Sin.
> O supporter of arms, who determines battles,
> O possessor of all divine power, who wears the
> crown of dominion,
> O Lady, glorious is thy greatness; over all the gods
> it is exalted.
>
> Anu, Enlil and Ea have made thee high; among the
> gods they have caused thy dominion to be
> great.
> They have made thee high among all the Igigi;
> they have made thy position pre-eminent.
> At the thought of thy name heaven and earth
> tremble.
> The judgment of the people in truth and righteous-
> ness thou indeed dost decide.
> Thou regardest the oppressed and mistreated; daily
> thou causest them to prosper.
>
> O deity of men, goddess of women, whose designs
> no one can conceive,
> Where thou dost look, one who is dead lives; one
> who is sick rises up;
> The erring one who sees thy face goes aright.
> I have cried to thee, suffering, wearied and distres-
> sed, as thy servant.

See me O my Lady; accept my prayers.
Faithfully look upon me and hear my supplication.
Promise my forgiveness and let thy spirit be
    appeased.

I toss about like flood-water, which an evil wind
    makes violent.
My heart is flying; it keeps fluttering like a bird of
    heaven.
I mourn like a dove night and day.
I am beaten down, and so I weep bitterly.
With "Oh" and "Alas" my spirit is distressed.
I—what have I done, O my god and my goddess?
Like one who does not fear my god and goddess I
    am treated.[31]

The supplicant then goes on to describe the dreadful
things that are happening to him: 'sickness, headache,
loss and destruction' are provided for him, the anger,
choler and indignation of gods and men are visited upon
him, and he is expecting 'dark days, gloomy months and
years of trouble'. His chapel is silent as are his house, his
gate and his fields. His family is scattered, his roof
broken up, and he himself is dressed in sackcloth,
pursued by enemies. Even his god has 'turned to the
sanctuary of another'. But Ishtar's devotee insists that
he cannot be accused of deserting his beloved Lady:

(But) I have paid heed to thee, my Lady; my
    attention has been turned to thee.
To thee have I prayed; forgive my debt.
Forgive my sin, my iniquity, my shameful deeds
    and my offence.

How long, O my Lady, wilt thou be angered so
    that thy face is turned away?

> How long, O my Lady, wilt thou be infuriated so
>   that thy spirit is enraged?[32]

It was clearly very uncomfortable to have Ishtar's
wrath visited upon one, and only her forgiveness and
favour would restore prosperity. We do not know what
her supplicant's sins were, but he assures her that
whatever else he may have done, he has remained
faithful to her. Indeed he wishes her to show him mercy
so that others might follow her too:

> Let my prayers and my supplications come to thee.
> Let thy great mercy be upon me.
> Let those who see me in the street magnify thy
>   name.
> As for me, let me glorify thy divinity and thy might
>   before the black-headed (people), [saying]
> Ishtar indeed is exalted; Ishtar indeed is queen;
> The Lady indeed is exalted; the Lady indeed is
>   queen.
>
> Irnini, the valorous daughter of Sin, has no rival.[33]

The followers of Ishtar may have felt obliged to
proclaim that she had no rival. To be untrue to Ishtar
was evidently dangerous, bringing dreadful calamities.
Yet Ishtar did have a rival, one whose claims to greatness
were far more splendid even than hers, one whose
transcendence, authority, compassion and power were
incomparably grander and one who ultimately not only
defeated her, but changed the face of history. The name
of that rival was Yahweh.

Chapter Three

Yahweh and the Queen of Heaven

Yahweh was the God of the ancient Hebrews—a Semitic tribe who first moved into Palestine around the beginning of the second millenium BC, but only settled there during the Early Iron Age (c 1200–900 BC). They settled in lands where the worship of the goddess and her baals or lords was a very ancient tradition, and the early centuries of their history are filled with the rivalry and conflicting claims of Yahweh and this Great Mother Goddess. As we have seen, the male sky gods were often too distant and uninterested in their people and the goddess therefore received the strongest devotion. Both supreme and lesser gods and goddesses, however, were prepared to play their part in the pantheon of deities and in the vegetation rites of the people. They acknowledged and depended upon each other's existence, battled over ultimate authority and interchanged their roles. Yahweh, God of the Hebrews was an altogether different being.

He claimed to be the one and only true universal God, beside whom all other gods and goddesses were as mere pieces of wood and stone. His first commandment to the Hebrews was, 'You shall have no other gods before me' (Ex. 20:3). He would not allow any 'graven image' of himself, and he would not acknowledge the efficacy of any other deity. He transcended all sexual characteristics, although he was addressed in masculine terms.

Despite his transcendence over human categories, he did nevertheless compare himself with his creation, and he was intimately concerned with the daily lives of his people. He laid down detailed laws about their moral, political, economic, agricultural and religious behaviour. Although similar in many ways to the high sky gods and storm gods of surrounding tribes, the differences were telling. The prophets of Yahweh were bitterly opposed to the sexual prostitution of other nature religions, to their polytheism and to the human sacrifice which was still being practised while he was making himself known to his people. He was not a distant, otiose sky god. Although he ruled the heavens, his dwellings were graciously with his people on earth.

Yahweh tried to teach his people that there was only one God—transcendent, and all-embracing, who needed no consort, was not contained by his creation, and who was not dependent upon the fortunes of his people and their land. However, it took many long centuries and much agony for the Hebrews finally to comprehend the transcendent nature of their God, and to stop seeing him as a purely masculine tribal God who was only one among many.

Yahweh, as maker of heaven and earth, revealed himself to the Hebrews in a uniquely exclusive and detailed covenant. He promised great and beautiful things if the people kept his commandments:

> If you walk in my statutes and observe my commandments and do them, then I will give you your rains in their season, and the land shall yield its increase, and the trees of the field shall yield their fruit. And your threshing shall last to the time of vintage, and the vintage shall last to the time for sowing; and you shall eat your bread to the full, and dwell in your land securely. And I will give you

peace in the land, and you shall lie down, and none shall make you afraid; and I will remove evil beasts from the land, and the sword shall not go through your land. (Lev. 26:3–6)

Whereas the Babylonians, Assyrians, Egyptians—all neighbouring peoples—tried to control the fertility of the soil, the rains in their seasons, and the protection from wild beasts and natural disasters by means of the sacred marriage involving the human representatives of earth and sky; and whereas they tried to ensure political, economic and social stability through the incantation of ritual songs and stories, the Hebrews were promised all these things by their God if they only obeyed his commandments. If they did not obey, however, then they would have dreadful disasters showered upon them by a God who did not need to keep them prosperous to prove his existence:

But if you will not hearken to me, and will not do all these commandments . . . I will do this to you: I will appoint over you sudden terror, consumption, and fever that waste the eyes and cause life to pine away. And you shall sow your seed in vain, for your enemies shall eat it . . . and I will break the pride of your power, and I will make your heavens like iron and your earth like brass; and your strength shall be spent in vain, for your land shall not yield its increase, and the trees of the land shall not yield their fruit. (Lev. 26:14–20)

Yahweh was 'a jealous God' who would not tolerate his people worshipping graven images or likenesses of other deities. He promised vengeance to the third and fourth generation for those who disobeyed him in this, making it quite clear what his people should do about the religions already established in the lands into which they came:

> Observe what I command you this day . . . . Take heed of yourself, lest you make a convenant with the inhabitants of the land whither you go, lest it become a snare in the midst of you. You shall tear down their altars, and break their pillars, and cut down their Asherim (for you shall worship no other God, for the Lord, whose name is Jealous, is a jealous God), lest you make a convenant with the inhabitants of the land . . . and you take of their daughters for your sons, and their daughters play the harlot after their gods and make your sons play the harlot after their gods. (Ex. 34:11–16)

Despite the magnificent promises of Yahweh and the violence of his threats, the people of Israel continually abandoned him and worshipped other gods and goddesses, especially the Great Goddess Astarte-Ishtar. It was as if they could only conceive of their God as a purely masculine, male deity who therefore needed a female counterpart and escort. Or perhaps they worshipped other gods and goddesses as a sort of insurance policy in case Yahweh turned out not to be all-powerful after all! Although the Hebrew men had been warned not to marry any non-Hebrew women, many of them did. These women came from the lands of the goddess and were very reluctant to depart from their religion and worship Yahweh. As Yahweh predicted, they frequently led their husbands away from the pure worship of Yahweh and encouraged them to show devotion to the Great Goddess and her consorts. Even King Solomon himself, who should have been such an outstanding example to his people, was a lover of foreign women. He had seven hundred wives and three hundred concubines—all foreign. We are told that these wives proved ultimately to be a snare:

> For when Solomon was old his wives turned away his heart after other gods; and his heart was not wholly true to the Lord his God, as was the heart of David his father. For Solomon went after Ashtoreth the goddess of the Sidonians, and after Milcom the abomination of the Ammonites.
>
> (I Kgs. 11:4–5)

Solomon also put up shrines to these foreign gods and goddesses—'And so he did for all his foreign wives, who burned incense and sacrificed to their gods.' Yahweh was very angry with Solomon, and promised to tear his kingdom from him except for one tribe which would be kept for the sake of David and Jerusalem. But long before Solomon's time the children of Israel had been led astray by foreign religions. A large portion of the Old Testament is taken up with stories of the attempts of Yahweh and his prophets to rid the Hebrews of their idolatry and apostasy, their 'unfaithfulness' to him.

The leader Gideon was told by God to 'pull down the altar of Baal which your father has and cut down the Asherah that is beside it' (Judg. 6:25). The priest Samuel instructed the whole house of Israel that they must return to the Lord their God and 'put away the foreign gods and the Ashtaroth from among you' (I Sam. 7:3). The dramatic contest between Elijah and the prophets and priestesses of Baal and Asherah was an attempt to prove once and for all the superiority of Yahweh. It was a sign of how strong was the opposition that the one God should have been set in contest with a mere baal. The expectation was that the silence from the baalim and the miracle of fire from Yahweh would finally convince the people that Yahweh was the one and only God. Yet despite Yahweh's great triumph, his prophet Elijah fled in terror from the revenge of Queen Jezebel, herself a staunch follower of Asherah. So greatly did he fear her wrath and power that when he escaped he pleaded with God to allow him to die. Jezebel had put to death so many of Yahweh's prophets that Elijah thought he alone was left alive.

Despite the unending pleas, reprimands, contests and threats of Yahweh and his servants, the people of Israel refused to abandon their other gods and goddesses. In the end the warnings of disaster in the face of disobedience came true. The prophet Ahijah had warned Jeroboam, successor to Solomon that 'the Lord will smite Israel, as a reed is shaken in the water, and root up Israel out of this good land which he gave to their fathers, and scatter them beyond the Euphrates because they have made their Asherim, provoking the Lord to anger' (1 Kgs. 14:15). The Asherim were the sacred pillars or poles of the Mother Goddess, stylized representations of a sacred tree, and were often worshipped as the goddess. In 721 BC, because of their failure to keep God's commandments, ten out of the twelve tribes of Israel were conquered by the Assyrians and exiled from the land which God had given them, never to be heard of again:

> And this was so, because the people of Israel had sinned against the Lord their God . . . and walked in the customs of the nations whom the Lord alone drove out before the people of Israel . . . they set up for themselves pillars and Asherim on every high hill and under every green tree. (2 Kgs. 17:7–10)

The dreadful fate of these ten tribes prompted King Josiah of the southern tribes of Judah—the remaining two—to instigate drastic reforms in his kingdom. Details of these reforms reveal just how deeply the goddess worship had encroached on the monotheism

and morality of the Hebrew religion as originally laid
down by Yahweh. Even the sacred temple itself had
been defiled with statues of Baal and Asherah, idolatrous
priests and male cult prostitutes:

> And the King commanded Hilkiah, the high priest
> . . . to bring out of the temple of the Lord all the
> vessels made for Baal, for Asherah, and for all the
> host of heaven; . . . And he deposed the idolatrous
> priests whom the kings of Judah had ordained to
> burn incense in the high places . . . those also who
> burned incense to Baal, to the sun, and the moon,
> and the constellations and all the host of the
> heavens. And he broke down the houses of the male
> cult prostitutes which were in the house of the
> Lord, where the women wove hangings for the
> Asherah. (2 Kgs. 23:4–7)

Despite all these efforts 'the Lord did not turn from
the fierceness of his great wrath', and the Queen of
Heaven continued to attract the loving attentions of the
Hebrew people. The prophet Jeremiah came across
many signs that her religion was as strong as ever. He
was dismayed to discover that in Jerusalem itself 'the
children gather wood, the fathers kindle fire and the
women knead dough to make cakes for the Queen of
Heaven' (Jer. 7:18). Yahweh's hurt, grief and anger
became inconsolable. Even the beloved tribe of Judah
would not stay faithful to him. He resolved that they too
must be exiled to teach them their lesson:

> My grief is beyond healing,
> my heart is sick within me . . .
> O that my head were waters,
> and my eyes a fountain of tears,
> that I might weep day and night . . .
>
> (Jer. 8:18, 9:1)

In 586 BC the remaining two tribes of Judah were attacked by the foreign King Nebuhcadrezzar. Jerusalem was sacked, the temple burned and the people taken into captivity. In time they learned their lesson, and when eventually they returned from their exile in Babylon the goddess worship was dead. But she did not go without a struggle. A few people had escaped capture, and fled to Egypt where they continued baking bread for the Queen of Heaven, burning incense to her and pouring out libations in her honour. When challenged by the now aged Jeremiah they retorted that they were determined to go on worshipping her:

> Then all the men who knew that their wives had offered incense to other gods, and all the women who stood by, a great assembly, all the people who dwelt in Pathros in the land of Egypt, answered Jeremiah: 'As for the word which you have spoken to us in the name of the Lord, we will not listen to you. But we will do everything that we have vowed, burn incense to the queen of heaven and pour out libations to her, as we did, both we and our fathers, our kings and our princes in the cities of Judah and in the streets of Jerusalem; for we had plenty of food and prospered and saw no evil. But since we left off burning incense to the queen of heaven and pouring out libations to her, we have lacked everything and have been consumed by the sword and by famine.' And the women said, 'When we burned incense to the queen of heaven and poured out libations to her, was it without our husbands' approval that we made cakes for her bearing her image and poured out libations to her?'
> (Jer. 44:15–19)

Yahweh's reply to this final act of defiance was to bring catastrophe to these Egyptian exiles, leaving only a few to return to Judah. Jeremiah told all the people, and especially the women, that they could go on performing their vows and worshipping Ishtar, but they and their men must face the consequences. God promised to break down what he had built, tear up what he had planted and bring evil upon all flesh. In the end only a remnant of the tribe of Judah survived the exile and returned to the land which God had originally given them. They returned chastened, shaken and determined to keep the purity of their faith as Yahweh had commanded it. Their worship of the goddess had led to catastrophe.

i. *THE SHADOW OF THE GODDESS*

The battle between Yahweh and the Mother Goddess of the near east was one of the most bitter episodes in Jewish history. The Hebrews' failure to obey the commands of their God led to a degrading exile, the overrunning of their land by foreigners and the burning of their precious temple. The prophets had waged a war against the goddess from the beginning, for they knew that their God would not tolerate her presence. It is significant that the religion of the Great Mother was a nature religion, and that in the bible we are told that it was the women who took the initiative in the practice. The connection between the goddess, nature religions and women is an important one, for all three have in varying degrees been 'outlawed' by the Jewish and later Christian traditions. As theologian Rosemary Ruether has observed:

> This struggle between Yahwism and the religion of Canaan was one of the most important influences in shaping Old Testament religion. The Old Testament rejection of female symbols for God, and perhaps also of female religious leaders, probably

had something to do with this struggle against Canaanite religion, with its powerful goddess figures and its female-dominated ceremonies of worship.[1]

The Hebrews had a strong and, as it emerged, wholly justified fear of the power of the goddess. Something of the importance of their battle with the goddess comes across in the differences between the two accounts of creation in Genesis 1–3. One appears to have been written before the exile when the goddess was at the height of her power; the other was completed afterwards when she no longer had any influence.

The earlier story of creation is the one contained in Genesis chapters 2–3. Scholars believe it was written around the first half of the tenth century BC. This story of the garden of Eden, with its magical tree of life, its speaking serpent and its wilful woman was undoubtedly made up from a number of different sources, according to many commentators who have observed its literary seams. The story of Eden and the fall has a great many levels of meaning, and considerable psychological and spiritual subtlety. It helps to explain some of the imponderables of human existence, such as the pain of childbirth, and the hardships of tilling the soil. However, there is one particularly interesting aspect to this tale which is highly relevant to our study of the goddess.

One of the most ancient symbols of the Great Goddess in the near east, Crete, and the Aegean was the serpent. In Egypt the association was so close that the hieroglyph for 'goddess' was a cobra. At Knossos the Minoan Snake-Goddess had a shrine in which she was depicted with three snakes coiled round her, a fourth in her right hand, and two more round her waist and hips. This cult went back to the Early Minoan Period of around 2500 BC—long before the story of Eve. There is a statuette which dates back to 3000 BC which portrays the Snake-Goddess holding two snakes high in her hands. In Apuleius's tale Isis is described with 'vipers rising from the left-hand and right-hand partings of her hair'. Ishtar was sometimes portrayed as covered with scales like a snake, or sitting on the throne of heaven, holding a staff round which were coiled two serpents.[2] As Georges Contenau tells us in *Everyday Life in Babylon and Assyria*, '. . . Ishtar, as the goddess who makes the corn to grow has a serpent as her companion, to emphasise her character as an earth deity.'[3]

The serpent was associated with immortality, magic, wisdom, prophecy and healing, as well as with evil and death. Its ability to shed its skin gave it this reputation for immortality and magic and the hallucinatory effect of its bite (if survived) may be the reason for its connection with wisdom and prophecy. Even in the story of the brazen serpent it was associated with healing. Its dwelling in the depths of the earth led to its association with fertility, chthonic powers and the underworld. The writers of the story of Eden would have been aware of these associations. As Samuel Hooke points out (in *Peake's Commentary on the Bible*), 'the Hebrew writers . . . did not invent a symbolism to express the various aspects of the divine activity, but took what lay ready to their hand, the material which they had inherited as part of their early cultural contacts, and transformed it into the vocabulary of the divine speech'.[4] He goes on to say that, although aware of the positive symbolism of the serpent in other cultures, for the writer of the Eden story the knowledge it represented was evil because it was associated with natural wisdom and magic: 'The serpent with his magic knowledge, his promises of life and fertility, was the fitting symbol of the guile which would lure men into the ways of death, away from the one truly good God, the only source of life and the only lawful object of knowledge.'[5] The goddess, with her serpent symbol was not a lawful object of knowledge and, as Hooke remarks, in the story of Adam and Eve's fall from grace through the enticements of the serpent, we see the Hebrew writer 'making skilful use of the old myths, the guile of the serpent, the gods' jealousy of man, and representing the serpent as offering to man the enticing prospect of vital knowledge which was being withheld by Yahweh through jealousy.'[6] As we have seen, Yahweh was indeed 'a jealous God' and could not accept any unfaithfulness from his people. The hypnotic charm of the ancient goddess worship was a serious threat to him.

The story of the garden of Eden told the people of Israel how the woman's openness to the guile and seduction of the serpent brought God's curse upon all humanity. Historically speaking, the Goddess Astarte-Ishtar, whose followers cried 'Irnini hath not a rival. My lady hath no rival', and who, like Yahweh, appeared to visit destruction and despair on those who disobeyed her, continued to find followers among the foreign women of Israel and they in turn persuaded their husbands to pay homage to her too. Adam and Eve were expelled from the garden of Eden because of their disobedience; Israel and Judah were expelled from the promised land because of their unfaithfulness. The similarity is remarkable, and not without significance.[7]

Of course this is not the only message of the second account of creation. It is undoubtedly not its main message, nor was it an obvious one, yet the parallels are there. Gerhard von Rad, commenting on the meaning of the name 'Eve' *(hawwah)* observes that this second naming after the name 'woman' is a recognisable 'seam' between two traditions. There is considerable speculation about the significance of this second name. Fascinatingly, von Rad says that 'The Aramaic word *hēwyā*

(serpent), has led to the supposition that at the basis of
the narrative there is a very different older form, in
which only three acting partners appear: God, man, and
a (chthonian) serpent deity.'⁸ As he says, there is
nothing palpable to justify such a theory and yet, as
John Gibson of Edinburgh University points out,
although the writers of the story were at pains to make it
clear that the serpent was just another of God's
creatures, nevertheless they used the name *nachash* to
describe him,⁹ the same word used to describe the great
evil monster of the deep, Leviathan.

In some other parts of the bible Leviathan comes
across as the powerful adversary of Yahweh. Yahweh
proves his might by slaying Leviathan, just as Marduk
slew Tiamat:

> Yet God my King is from of old
> working salvation in the midst of the earth.
> Thou didst divide the sea by thy might;
> Thou didst break the heads of the dragons on the
>   waters.
> Thou didst crush the heads of Leviathan,
> Thou didst give him as food for the creatures of the
>   wilderness.   (Ps. 74:12–14)

In the Ugaritic texts of ancient pre-Israelite Canaan,
the God Baal also fights the dragon of the sea:

> Have I not slain Sea, beloved of El?
> Have I not annihilated River, the great God?
> Have I not muzzled the Dragon, holding her in a
>   muzzle?
> I have slain the Crooked Serpent,
> The Foul-fanged with seven heads.

As Gibson has pointed out, by using the word
nachash to describe the serpent in Eden, the writers
introduce the idea that there was a force of evil in the

world which had resisted Yahweh from the beginning of time. It may well be that they saw this force of evil as the deeply threatening and all-powerful serpent-goddess whose worship was dominant in the near east, and whose seductive charms undid the Hebrews.

As we saw, by the time the Hebrews returned from exile, the goddess's power among them had been eradicated. She no longer appears in the pages of the bible as a threat to the monotheism of Yahweh. This is reflected in the very different account of creation which was edited after the exile by the priests. In the story of creation in Genesis I there are no mythological monsters, no talking serpents, no trees of life and no disobedient women. Order has been established, rebellions have been quelled, and peace reigns. All traces of polytheistic thought have been rooted out and the account shows the mark of a theology which has been carefully considered, reformed and purified. It is generally recognised to be more scholarly, abstract, and theological than the folk-tale of Genesis 2–3.

There are many pointers to this reformed theological thinking: for instance, there is no hint of any battle between God and any other deity; there is no colourful and powerful adversary such as Leviathan the serpent; even the sun and moon are not named, but only referred to as the greater and lesser lights, (earlier they had been worshipped as independent deities, even in the temple of Jerusalem itself). By giving them no individual names, the priests emphasised that they had no existence independent of God. Similarly, despite the obvious parallels between the Babylonian story of Marduk conquering Tiamat, goddess of the primeval sea, and the God of Genesis keeping down the chaotic forces of the deep, the writers do not give the concept of chaos a separate identity. There seems to be little doubt that the Hebrew word for the deep, *tehōm* is connected with the

Babylonian Tiamat, but it has no separate existence in
Genesis I, whereas in other parts of the bible the floods
are given a voice and an identity:

> The floods have lifted up, O Lord,
> The floods have lifted up their voice,
> The floods lift up their roaring.
> Mightier than the thunders of many waters,
> Mightier than the waves of the sea,
> the Lord on high is mighty!   (Ps. 93:3–4)

ii. *THE PATRIARCHAL SPIRIT AND HINTS OF TRANSCENDENCE*

Although in many ways unique, the Hebrew religion
clearly reflects its times. It is clear even in Genesis I that
it was a patriarchal religion which, like the religions of
surrounding countries, reflected the masculine drive for
mastery. Marduk divided up the Primeval Ocean,
Tiamat; Baal slew Sea, River, the dragon and the
crooked serpent, and Yahweh was victorious over
Leviathan and the mighty floods. Despite the many
differences, the Babylonian, Canaanite and Hebrew
stories do share the same imperative to create order out
of chaos—an imperative which was evident in various
parts of Mesopotamia. The overpowering surge of the
floods of the ocean symbolised the overpowering threat
of too much identification with and bondage to the
natural world.

The religion of Israel taught that almighty Yahweh
was the maker and controller of the seasons, that he
alone had brought harmony out of confusion. The
hostility to the nature religions of the goddess must have
been so strong partly because they seemed to teach too
little of humanity's ability to moderate the instinctive
forces of nature. The desire to control, master and
penetrate the mysteries of nature and of our own nature

has been a very important factor in human development. As psychologist Sukie Colegrave has pointed out, when this more masculine consciousness began to develop,

> . . . it generated a revolution in humanity's relationship to its environment without which individual becoming and Self-knowledge might have been impossible . . . The foundation of relative material security permitted the emergence of human cultures in a way hitherto prohibited by the incessant movement and unpredictable survival characteristic of the pre-patriarchal epoch. Philosophy, art and science, together with all methods of developing and exploring our inner worlds, depend on a certain degree of independence from nature's rule.[10]

Today, of course, we face the disastrous consequences of too much independence from nature, a growing ignorance of her ways, and the dominance of masculine values, but as Sukie Colegrave says, there was a time when such independence was vital.

In Genesis 1:28 we are told that God commanded the man and woman whom he had just made to fill the earth, subdue it, and have dominion over every living thing. There are many today who find this command offensive, smacking of a patronising attitude of lordship, even violence towards nature. However, if we see this verse in the context of the whole bible, and particularly in the historical context in which it was written after the exile, we will see that such an accusation is unfounded.

The writers of Genesis 1 could not possibly have been advocating an exploitative treatment of the earth and its inhabitants. They had already learnt that such an attitude was unacceptable to God. God had given his people explicit laws concerning the correct treatment of both the land and the animals. The most important of these was the sabbath year—a year of rest for the land every seventh year to allow the soil to renew its fertility. This was a form of fallowing, an ancient method of soil conservation. Despite dire warnings of the consequences of failing to keep this law, the Hebrews did not observe it, just as they ignored God's commandments regarding other things. It seems that they misused the land God had given them and in some parts of the bible we are told that the prime reason why the Hebrews were exiled was to allow the land to rest:

> He took into exile in Babylon those who had escaped from the sword, and they became servants to him and to his sons until the establishment of the Kingdom of Persia, to fulfil the word of the Lord by the mouth of Jeremiah, until the land had enjoyed its sabbaths. All the days it lay desolate it kept sabbath, to fulfil seventy years.
>
> (2 Chron. 36:20–21)

When the Jews returned from exile they did try to keep the sabbath year, although they were less successful in this than in ridding themselves of the goddess. It is most unlikely therefore, as we can see, that the priestly writers of Genesis 1 would deliberately represent God as commanding his people to trample on and exploit the land all over again. It is perhaps significant that in the book of Genesis, the command to have dominion over the earth actually leads into the story of the garden of Eden. In the garden the masculine drive to control nature was kept in check and the man and woman were as much part of nature as masters of it. They were at one with God's other creatures and plants, they tended the soil creatively and brought about a harmonious balance between the human instinct to create and the natural order. The masculine drive for mastery does not necessarily lead to exploitation, manipulation and pollution. If there is a balance between respect for nature's own wisdom and the intelligent controlling of her forces, then neither nature nor humanity will be the victim.

God was deeply connected with his creation: he revealed his pleasure through abundant harvests and his displeasure through droughts, pestilence and floods. He was intimately concerned with the careful management of his world. He taught his people that fertility came from good husbandry and care for nature's needs, rather than from vegetation cults and promiscuous rites. The Hebrew religion was profoundly in touch with the rhythms and cycles of the times and seasons, but not in bondage to them.

Yahweh taught his people both to be a part of nature and to penetrate her mysteries. In this he combined both the masculine and feminine spirit and showed that he was God of nature and of all history.

The God of Israel was lord and creator of both heaven and earth. He was not a distant, uninvolved, otiose sky-father, he had something to say about every detail of the lives of his people. Nor was he so identified with and contained by his creation and its fertility that he could be compared to an earth-mother. Yahweh transcended both earth-mother and sky-father, he laid down the laws of the universe, including the fertility of the soil, and the revolution of the planets. Heaven was his throne and earth his footstool.

Yahweh was no mere Iron Age Marduk, a purely male tribal god fighting a hostile goddess, he combined both masculine and feminine qualities in his character, and transcended them in a way which was unique in Mesopotamia. As E O James has said,

> . . . in Mesopotamia, the concept of deity was never conceived in terms of a single transcendental

Being as the author and ground of all existence,
devoid of anthropomorphic and sexual characteristics and dependence upon the rise and fall of the
city or territory with which he was especially
associated . . . this achievement among the Semites
was reserved for the Hebrews.[11]

At first Yahweh's people could not grasp the greatness
of his claims and saw him just as their god among many
gods and goddesses. But in time something of his
mysteriously transcendent nature did penetrate, as the
creation story of Genesis 1 shows.

By using the name Elohim to describe God in the first
account of creation, the priestly writers conveyed their
understanding of God's transcendence. Elohim—the
'plural of majesty'—was in common use in pre-Israelite
Palestine and Babylonia. It described the head of the
pantheon, whether god or goddess. Its feminine application is demonstrated in 1 Kings 11:5 where we are told
that Solomon went after Ashtoreth, goddess (*elohim*) of
the Sidonians. By using this name for God, the writers
were not only acknowledging that in the beginning the
name Yahweh was not known, but also making a clear
statement about his supremacy over all deities, and over
all categories of masculine and feminine. As Walther
Eichrodt confirms, 'By choosing this particular name,
which as the epitome of all-embracing divine power
excludes all other divinity, (the writer) was able to
protect his cosmogony from any trace of polytheistic
thought and at the same time describe the Creator God
as the absolute Ruler and only Being whose will carries
any weight.'[12]

The ultimate expression of God's transcendence over
human categories as well as his identification with them
comes in verses 26 and 27 of Genesis 1, where Elohim
said, 'Let us make man in our image, after our like-

ness . . . . So God created man in his own image, in the image of God he created him; male and female he created them.' The other religions of the ancient near east had created the gods and goddesses in their own image—in the image of man and woman. The priests of the Hebrew religion finally understood that the universal creator had made man and woman 'after our likeness'—that is in the image of *God*. This single statement perfectly expressed both God's transcendence over and his total identification with his people. He could not be limited by the sexual differences he himself had created; he could not be depicted by any stone or wooden image; his image was in living man and woman. But it was in them *equally*. Both individually and together they were made in the image of the one true God.

The statement 'male and female created he them' not only shows God's transcendence over sexual stereotypes, but also the human transcendence over stereotypes and the equality of woman and man in God's sight. The contrast between the theology of Genesis 1 regarding the relationship between man and woman and the position presented in the story of Adam and Eve is very striking.

We shall see that it has been made much of over the years. The purified and scholarly minds of the priestly writers produced a statement in verse 27 of great beauty and simplicity; a statement so radical in the equality it granted to women that its meaning has been hotly contested for millenia. By saying 'in the image of God he created him; male and female he created them', the writers made it clear that it was not only man who was in the image of God, nor had God created a hemaphrodite. He had created humankind as a man and a woman— male and female—each made in the image of God, and each capable of experiencing in him or herself something of both the masculine and feminine qualities of their maker. So Emil Brunner emphasised:

> That is the immense double statement, of a lapidary simplicity, so simple indeed that we hardly realise that with it a vast world of myth and Gnostic speculation, of cynicism and asceticism, of the deification of sexuality and fear of sex completely disappears.[13]

In the countries of the ancient near east, the sacred marriage of sky-father and earth-mother, acted out by human representatives, was an expression of people's awareness of the need for both masculine and feminine forces in the creation of life. It also expressed their desire to see the rain of heaven mingled with the fertile earth to produce rich harvests of food. The implicit and explicit androgyny of many of the great gods and goddesses was the inner expression of the same truth. However, as we have seen, the marriage was seldom one of equals and was often a violent and brutal affair. Either the male gods were butchering, raping and usurping the goddesses, or the goddesses were totally eclipsing their young male escorts, requiring their death each year as the seasons changed, and dominating the partnership. Many lesser deities were unequivocally male or female and their battles were tribal battles.

At first Yahweh, God of Israel, was very much part of these struggles between the different gods and goddesses, proving his authority and power against theirs. In the beginning his followers only saw him as their own god among others. His masculinity was emphasised to make his identity quite clear in the midst of the land of the goddess. However, after many battles, competitions, harsh words and dreadful catastrophes, something of the mysterious nature of the one true God, maker of heaven and earth was understood: Genesis 1 paid tribute to this.

It took a long time for the Hebrew people to grasp what their God was telling them—that he was even greater than the androgynous Great Mother, that he was both father and mother to his people, that they needed no cultic sacred marriage to express the opposites of life, that these were in each individual person who, made in the image of God, could know both feminine feelings and masculine power, in him or herself. As Brunner said, there has been a vast amount of speculation over this mystery of life, not only in the near east, but all over the world. The search for the meaning of the opposites, and the drive to achieve their union, has concentrated the minds of some of the world's wisest men and women since time began. It was considered to be a mystery of nature worth penetrating, for it seemed to express the very essence of creation and the creator, and transcended both matriarchal and patriarchal dogma.

Chapter Four

The marriage of heaven and earth

The attempt to understand the phenomenon of the duality of life, which is one in essence but two in manifestation, has been at the heart of some of the world's greatest religions. As we saw in the previous chapter, the near eastern peoples strove to express their understanding of the balance of masculine and feminine through a sacred cultic marriage of sky-father and earth-mother. The Great Mother's androgyny was the inner expression of the same truth, as was Yahweh's transcendence over sexual stereotypes. But it was not only in the near east that these insights had an important part to play in religious and philosophical thought.

Since earliest times, people have looked around them and seen two creative and uniting forces at work. At first these were both understood to be contained in the one unit, like the Great Mother, then they were divided into male and female, but in the higher deities they were reunited to express their all-embracing authority and power. St. Paul wrote that 'Ever since the creation of the world [God's] invisible nature, namely his eternal power and deity, has been clearly perceived in the things that have been made' (Rom. 1:20). Different civilisations have had different perceptions of God as revealed in his works, but very many have shared the common view that God's plan for creation was a harmonious marriage of opposites, a happy union of sky and soil, and a close communion between God and humanity, spirit and matter, nature and humanity. Traditions have held that a discordant relationship between these opposites brings stultification, misunderstanding, strife, violence. Today we should also add ecological disaster. Much time has been spent defining the meaning of these opposites, absorbing them into life and aiding their union. We note the more influential definitions:

i. *YIN AND YANG*

One of the oldest books in the world is the ancient Chinese Oracle of Change called the *I Ching*. Although the wisdom it embodies has been expanded and redefined over many centuries by great philosophers such as Lao-tse and Confucius, its origins are believed to lie as far back as the 4th millenium BC. In this ancient philosophy of life, earth was seen as feminine and heaven as masculine, just as in so many other civilisations around the world. The whole of life and the universe was understood to be divided into two complementary poles, represented by heaven and earth, and given the names 'yin' and 'yang'. It was not considered necessary to act out this truth in an external animistic marriage such as that of Canaanite religion. According to Chinese wisdom, this was an inner perception.

There were very many qualities attributed to the yang and yin. Amongst other things, yang was warm, dry, masculine, active, positive, expansive, competitive, rational and analytical. It was associated with the sun, daytime and heaven. Yin on the other hand was moist, cool, feminine, passive, negative, contractive, co-operative, intuitive and unitive. It was associated with the moon, nightime and with earth. It is highly significant that these attributes were not defined as belonging to sex or gender—male or female—but to qualities—masculine and feminine. Each person, whether man or woman, was seen to have a balance of yin and yang within his or her nature. Each part of creation was understood to contain that harmonious balance. This point cannot be emphasised enough.

The *I Ching* is made up of sixty four hexagrams, each of which has a unique combination of yang and yin lines. These were believed to reflect the interchanging cycles and balances within the whole of creation, from the ebb and flow of the tides, to the motions of the planets and the fortunes of humanity. All of nature was seen to be in a constant state of flux, ever changing into its opposite, for 'The yang having reached its climax retreats in favour of the yin; the yin having reached its climax, retreats in favour of the yang.'[1] The cycles of the universe revolved around these dual poles of existence, returning to the source which was the still point and recommencement.

The first hexagram of the *I Ching* represents the creative power of masculine activity. It is called 'Creativity':

> Great is the power of primal creativity. The source of all things, it embodies the significance of Heaven. Clouds move and rain falls, and all things develop in their appropriate forms . . .
>
> Creativity changes and transforms, in order that everything might attain its true nature in accordance with the will of Heaven. Great harmony can then prevail.[2]

The second hexagram is called 'quiescence' and represents the all-embracing productiveness of the feminine pole:

> Great is the power of quiescence. It obediently receives the forces of creativity and all things owe their birth to it.

71

> It enfolds everything in its embrace, and comple-
> ments the unlimited power of creativity. Through
> its shining abundance all things are able to reach
> their full development.[3]

It was basic to Chinese yin-yang philosophy that
neither the masculine nor the feminine pole was
dominant, that they were always in harmonious communion with one another. In hexagram 11, where they
are perfectly balanced, the title is 'Peace': in hexagram
12, where they block each other's path, the title is
'Stagnation'. Stagnation is the worst possible condition,
for it denies life, and is out of tune with the dynamic
rhythms and cycles of nature. As the *I Ching* says,
'Stagnation springs from the fact that Heaven and Earth
are not in communion with each other, and that in
consequence all things do not intermingle. The high and
the low, superiors and inferiors, do not communicate
with one another, and there are no well-governed states
to be seen anywhere.'
The failure of heaven and earth, masculine and
feminine, yang and yin, to be in harmony with each
other would lead to confusion, disorder and stagnation
throughout the whole created order, even of government itself. But when the yin and yang forces were in a
happy, creative, harmonious relationship then peace and
confidence reigned throughout the land and mighty
things could be accomplished. The purpose of the *I
Ching* was to provide a guide to these forces of
withdrawal and return, activity and passivity, initiative
and quiescence, for 'the superior man strives to align
himself with the set of the celestial tides, thus attracting
good fortune and supreme success'.[4] When a person was
in tune with the universal rhythms and the rhythms of
his or her own body, mind and spirit, then he or she
would be living in harmony with the will of Heaven. To

be out of tune would lead to misfortune and unavoidable distress. However, the message of the *I Ching* is that everything changes, and even misfortune can give way to joy.

When we remember the battles and rivalries in the near east between the earth-mother and sky-father, and the Great Mother and Yahweh, it is worth noting that in Chinese philosophy there was no possible rivalry or hierarchy between yin and yang. They were not conflicting opposites, but composite parts of one whole. Each is of supreme importance and equal value. It is inconceivable that anything could be solely yin or yang—masculine or feminine, heaven or earth, active or passive—everything is always a mixture of both. The symbol which depicts this profound truth is the *T'ai Chi*. In the *T'ai Chi* there are two halves shaped rather like embryos thrusting each other round in an ever circling motion. Although distinct and separate, each contains part of the other in itself and this is the significance of the spot at the centre of each half. J C Cooper explains:

> The yin-yang symbol, the *Ta Ki* [T'ai Chi], depicts the perfect balance of the two great forces in the universe; each has within it the embryo of the other power, implying that there is no exclusively masculine or feminine nature, but that each contains the germ of the other and there is continual alternation. The two powers are contained within the circle of cyclic revolution and dynamism of the totality. The whole forms the Cosmic Egg, the primordial Androgyne, the perfection of balance and harmony, the pure essence which is neither yet both. The two forces are held together in tension but not in antagonism, as mutually interdependent partners; one in essence, but two in manifestation.[5]

73

ii. *A QUESTION OF NUMBERS*

Plato once said that the number two was meaningless for it implied a relationship which would always lead on to a third factor. The understanding of the significance of numbers and their relationships was another very ancient tradition dating back long before Plato. It was based on a system of knowledge related to a canon of measurements, universally recognised to have cosmic significance. These measurements were a mathematical demonstration of natural law and were frequently applied to architecture, music, art, and even literature. Certain numbers, measurements and geometric shapes were believed to hold a mystic power and universal truth. The initiates who knew the vital ratios could give their work and words different levels of meaning by weaving into them the relevant numbers. This tradition is central to the *I Ching*, but can also be found in early Greek, Hebrew and Egyptian artefacts, documents and treasures, as well as in the works of many other civilisations.

There was a vast array of numbers which held great significance, but three are of special interest. These are 666, 1080, and their addition 1746. The most familiar number will probably be 666, being the 'number of the beast' in Revelation where it reads: 'This calls for wisdom: let him who has understanding reckon the number of the beast, for it is a human number, its number is six hundred and sixty-six.' (Rev. 13:18). John calls the number 666 'the number of a man' and this gives some clue as to its meaning. Both Greek and Hebrew letters can be read as numbers, for $(\alpha)=1$ $(\beta)=2$ etc in Greek and $(\aleph)=1, (\beth)=2$ etc in Hebrew. This gives the words a numerological significance as well as a literary one. Using this method the name of the Roman Emperor Caesar Nero added up to the number 666.

Nero persecuted Christians throughout his empire, torturing them and putting them to death. He may well have been the beast of Revelation with the number of a man.

The number 666 had a more universal meaning however than just the name of a cruel Emperor. This number represented absolute masculine energy; it symbolised the cosmic fire of the sun, with its creative, all-important life-giving power. It was light, energy, virility, intellect, consciousness and will. In its positive aspect, it mirrored hexagram 1 of the *I Ching*. But, it was only creative when in balance with other numbers. On its own, without the necessary checks, it would bring about destruction, violence, and holocaust by fire. As John Michell explains: 'Where the proportions are correct, the influence of the number 666 promotes fertility, gives life and colour, but where it becomes excessively dominant, the consequences are apparent in the tyranny of the self-willed governor, and in the development of a society obsessed with fantasies of violence, material wealth and power.'[6]

As history has shown, the Emperor Nero was a self-willed tyrant who destroyed Rome by fire. His masculine qualities had been allowed to dominate over the feminine and his lack of control led to holocaust.

In an article in *Spirals*, Richard Snead explains that the number 666 is related to the diameter of the hexagonal carbon ring and '. . . is an archtype of the sun (the 6 on the qabalistic Tree of Life, Tipharet) taken to the superlative degree. It is this sun-power which is released when the carbon ring is shattered in gunpowder or dynamite.'[7] The gunpowder, dynamite and nuclear weaponry of modern war are an expression of 666 at its most destructive.

The second number, 1080, was the exact opposite of 666. It represented the purely feminine attributes and was associated with the coolness of the moon, the fluidity of water, the cyclic rhythms of nature, instinctive powers, and the depths of the unconscious. The radius of the moon is 1080 miles. If 1080 was in balance it would bring spiritual and intuitive wisdom, prophetic powers, a sense of oneness with nature and the universe. It would be equivalent to hexagram 2 of the *I Ching*. But if 1080 was allowed to dominate, then the primordial powers of the unconscious would rise up and threaten stability. There would be too much fatalistic absorption into the rhythms and deterministic cycles of life, and too little awareness of individual separateness. If 1080 is not correctly balanced then as Michell says, '. . . the female, receptive spirit, 1080, withdraws into the earth, becomes stagnant and takes on the dark, malicious qualities of the elemental.'[8] Domination by 666 led to holocaust by fire: domination by 1080 would lead to destruction under the rising torrents of a flood.

The numbers 666 and 1080 when in harmonious communion with other numbers were extremely creative and equivalent to the positive aspects of yin and yang. However, when added to each other, this creativity became even greater, and produced a number of the utmost significance—the number of fusion, 1746. This was considered to be one of the most vital, symbolic and informative of numbers, for it represented the kingdom of heaven as found potentially in a grain of mustard seed. According to Gematria (the tradition which gave letters numerical equivalents) 1746 was the addition of the letters in the phrase—a grain of mustard seed *(kokkos sinapeōs)*. Ancient cosmology held that creation issued from the union of the two opposite forces of life—yin, yang; heaven, earth; masculine, feminine. The grain of mustard seed represented the Cosmic Egg, the Virgin Womb, the *T'ai Chi*, the union of the opposites in their primal state from which issued all creation. This was very well illustrated in the Japanese creation myth where the primal state was a mingling of In and Yo, heaven and earth; divine beings issued from the marriage of these opposites. Jesus himself likened the kingdom of heaven to the mustard seed which, although the smallest of seeds, had all the creative forces necessary inside its shell to produce the greatest of shrubs: 'With what can we compare the kingdom of God, or what parable can we use for it? It is like a grain of mustard seed, which, when sown upon the ground, is the smallest of all the seeds on earth; yet when it is sown it grows up and becomes the greatest of all shrubs, and puts forth large branches, so that the birds of the air can make nests in its shade' (Mk. 4:30–32).

iii. *THE ALCHEMICAL TRANSFORMATION*

The message of numerology was that God was behind the union of the dual poles of nature—their marriage was part of his plan for creation. The image of the tiny mustard seed suggested all the power, beauty and creative potential of the kingdom of heaven itself. People have tried to express their understanding of this truth in very many different ways: some have tried to convey the essence of the mystery through outward animistic and physical acts; others have spoken allegorically of a marriage of heaven and earth; yet others have seen it as a purely mystical, spiritual and psychological truth. One philosophical tradition which has been branded as heretical for its exploration of this mystery is alchemy.

Alchemy has often been caricatured as some sort of obscure, cranky, highly dubious practice of magical arts. This image has undoubtedly been encouraged by its practitioners who wished to protect its secrets from the ignorant and uninitiated. The popular picture of the crusty old alchemist, forever endeavouring to extract gold from base metal for his own gain and to further some devilish scheme is very far from the truth. Alchemy was an ancient system of knowledge which tried to comprehend the mysteries of life and creation. The alchemist's maxim was: 'as above, so below', an idea which can be found in many philosophical and religious traditions such as Platonism, Taoism, Buddhism; Jewish, Islamic and Christian mysticism. Alchemists believed that each particle of nature, each material object—whether animal, vegetable or mineral— was a microcosm of the divine macrocosm, and so contained a spark of the divine spirit. The earth was not an insensate conglomeration of mass, but had life and spirit. As the alchemist Basilius Valentinus explained:

> The earth is not a dead body, but is inhabited by a spirit that is its life and soul. All created things, minerals included, draw their strength from the earth spirit. The spirit is life, it is nourished by the stars, and it gives nourishment to all the living things it shelters in its womb. Through the spirit received from on high, the earth hatches the minerals in her womb as the mother her unborn child.[9]

The alchemists set themselves the task of finding and releasing spirit from the bondage of matter, but sought to do this on spiritual and psychological levels as well as the physical. The treasure they attempted to release was given a variety of names, all obscure. For instance it could be known as the Philosopher's Stone, the Philosopher's Gold, or the Son of the Philosopher. This magical and precious element emerged from the transformed matter. Its complexity was illustrated by the German alchemist Michael Maier who wrote: 'The sun is the image of God, the heart is the sun's image in man. . . . Gold is the sun's image in the Earth . . . (thus) God is known in the gold'.[10] The treasure which the alchemists sought was both God and gold.

The philosophy and practice of alchemy was based on very ancient knowledge. It is therefore fascinating to discover that a central feature was the balance of opposites, called the 'alchemical wedding' or the *mysterium coniunctionis*. This alchemical process involved analysing and separating the component parts of a substance or psyche, and then reassembling them in a more 'perfectly' harmonious way. It was almost as if they were re-enacting the creative work of God and it was this aspect of their work which gave to them the name of heretics.

As with the Chinese and the numerologists, the alchemists saw all of life divided into polarities, epitomised by 'masculine' and 'feminine'. These opposites were seen as antagonistic at first, but the alchemical process aimed to overcome their conflict and bring them together in a creative and complementary union. The Philosopher's Gold, the transformed substance, would only emerge once the analysed and separated components were 'remarried' in a perfect balance, the dual poles of heaven and earth, sun and moon, sulphur and quicksilver, queen and king were for them united in the figure of the androgyne. This represented the sacred marriage, the conciliation of opposites, humankind restored to wholeness. This bringing together of the two poles of nature was both a physical and spiritual goal—the transformation of matter and the transformation of the soul.

The spiritual wisdom of the balance of opposites has been appreciated in a great many of the high religions. Supreme deities have often been represented as androgynous as a sign of their all-embracing power. In the Hindu tradition, it is said that the god Śiva would be a corpse without his female counterpart, Sakti. Considerable energy is spent bringing about their union. One of Śiva's names is Śiva Matrbhutesvara—'Śiva who becomes a mother,' and in Assam he turns into a sacred buffalo cow as a sign of his maternal capacity. In Hindu Tantric tradition it is considered possible for a man and a woman so to purify themselves that the sexual act itself becomes a mystical, spiritual expression of the two forces of the universe—Śiva and Sakti made one.[11] There are many statues of Śiva/Sakti in India where their androgyny is physically depicted; there are also statues of a man and a woman in the act of union representing the sacred marriage of the eternal masculine and feminine principles, which statuary we trivialise at our peril.

iv. *ANIMUS AND ANIMA*

As we know, however, this truth did not always have to be expressed physically. The physical facts are only one aspect of this universal phenomenon. It was not necessary to build androgynous statues, enact sacred marriages, or take part in animistic cultic rites to emphasise the importance of an equal, harmonious marriage of opposites. The physical is only one level of the truth. It also has profound spiritual and psychological meaning. Taoist philosophy teaches that truth, far from being given a physical manifestation, could not even be named:

> The Tao that can be told is not the eternal Tao.
> The name that can be named is not the eternal name.
> The nameless is the beginning of heaven and earth.[12]

The harmony of masculine and feminine forces within the personality has been recognised throughout the ages to be a sign of great spiritual and psychological maturity and wholeness. As we have seen, Chinese philosophy, numerology, alchemy, religious and philosophical traditions have pointed to this ideal equality and harmony between the opposites, but the person who has done most this century to draw together these ancient traditions and develop a modern idea of the balance of psychic opposites is Carl Jung. He spent a large part of his life studying the meaning of the opposites and his last major work was devoted to the exploration of alchemical symbols in relation to them.[13]

Jung rediscovered the psychic power of traditional myths and symbols, and provided a way for us to re-establish contact with them through our dreams and fantasies. He was keenly conscious of what has been lost, warning that in our modern sophistication we have severed our connection with the wise messages of nature. The inner marriage of opposites, so vital for wholeness and health, has been hampered by our apparently overwhelming need to polarise spirit and matter, conscious and unconscious, intellect and instinct.

If we divorce ourselves from nature then we cut ourselves off from our own natures as well, for we are all part of God's creation and made according to the same plan: 'of the earth, earthy'. Just as the ancients saw patterns of withdrawal and return, seedtime and harvest, activity and passivity in nature, so these patterns are found in human beings too. Jung believed that it is of fundamental importance for each of us to find the meaning of the balance of opposites in our own psyche. He was profoundly aware of the need for this balance in an individual's emergence as a whole person. He called this process of growth towards wholeness 'individuation' and saw it as leading to the higher self. He likened it to the alchemical marriage of opposites which produced the Philosopher's Gold. Just as the alchemists separated and analysed components into their opposites in order to recompose them in a perfect union, so Jung encouraged his patients to analyse and distinguish the components of their psyche in order to come into a proper relationship with them and achieve psychological wholeness and maturity.

According to Jung, within each woman there is an undiscovered man, and within each man an undiscovered woman. The former he called the 'animus' and the latter the 'anima'. This inner opposite appears very frequently in our dreams, but can also be identified in traditional folk-tales and legends which have often been interpreted as symbolic descriptions of the inner life. The stories of Beauty and the Beast or Bluebeard's Castle, for instance, portray a girl's developing awareness of her own animus. The story of the teutonic Lorelei could be interpreted as a warning of the dangers of a man's negative anima, as indeed could the story of Eve itself. These psychic opposites within our own personality have great power over us both for good and ill. Our relationship to our animus or anima is determined at first by our relationship to our parents. A creative acknowledgement of the man or woman within can liberate our animus or anima to be an invaluable spiritual guide and guardian. But if the powerful force within is not recognised and accepted then it can wreak havoc in the personality, and 'possess' the individual by the strength of its repressed presence in the unconscious. Thus a proper awareness and balance of the masculine and feminine energies within each person is vital for health and growth.

Jung saw the anima as the personification of all the feminine aspects of a man's psyche. It was equivalent to the yin, to the second hexagram of the *I Ching*, or to the qualities of the number 1080. It brought him intuition, prophetic gifts, emotional openness, the ability to love, a sense of oneness with nature, and it provided the vital bridge between the conscious and the unconscious. A man's anima would bring him spirituality, insight and sensitivity if his relationship to it was open, balanced and accepted. If however he tried to repress or dominate his anima, it would emerge in more sinister ways. Negative relationships with the anima can lead to an over-emphasis on virility and sexual fantasies, neurotic over-intellectualism, a sense of unreality, over-sensitivity, pettiness and insecurity. The rejected anima works away in the unconscious, leading the man into real danger unless he faces his own feminine qualities and assimilates them into the rest of his character.

The masculine aspect of a woman's psyche is her animus. Masculinity can bring to her personality courage, initiative, creative power, active energy, leadership qualities, discernment and rational objectivity. Its equivalent is the yang pole of nature, the first hexagram of the *I Ching,* and the potency of the number 666. The animus is a spiritual guide and brings to a woman a sense of her own uniqueness and her ability to transcend nature and the rhythms of her own body. If her relationship to the animus is mature and balanced she will be a wise, strong, courageous woman, able to take initiative, combining the best of the feminine virtues with the best of the masculine. However, if a woman represses her animus, or does not attempt to understand it, she may well be unable to grow up, or may be bossy, opinionated, cold, ruthless and unfeeling. She may feel she has no worth, and is totally uncreative and uncultured. She may be dominating, aggressive, and competitive, intransigent about her own rightness. Like the repressed anima, the thwarted animus could lead a woman to her death.

One of today's leading interpreters of Jung's psychology is the analyst and author June Singer. She has not only helped to explain and clarify the meaning of Jung's work, but has also applied it to modern life. Although a great admirer and follower of his teaching, she is critical

83

of what appears to be some very sexist conclusions drawn by him. For instance, it would appear that Jung believed that the woman's masculine nature was to be developed not so much to make her courageous and give her strength, but to produce the seeds needed to fertilise the feminine aspect of the man! Jung wrote, 'Just as a man produces his work as a complete creation out of his inner feminine nature, so the inner masculine side of a woman produces creative seeds that can fertilise the feminine element in the man.'[14]

Singer is critical of this aspect of Jung's psychology. She believes that society today, with its new awareness of the need for equality between the sexes has, as she put it, finally lost patience with the idea of '. . . a frail and tiny ego differentiating itself, step by step, out of the boundless Self, finding its identity as man or woman, and in the process accepting the stereotype belonging to the gender role.'[15] As she says, Jung was writing sixty years ago when the idea of woman's subservience to man was openly held. Today, however, we have the opportunity for each person, man and woman, to find his or her hidden opposites without the straight-jacket of stereotyped roles. The search itself will lead both man and woman to a fulfilled, creative, and spiritually developed awareness of their potential. As Singer says, as we grow to understand the importance of the search for inner harmony and balance, so increasingly 'There are intimations of the Divine Self within ourselves, and the desire to experience more of this draws us forward with increasing energy and speed toward an inner unity.'[16]

Images of the Higher Self appear in our dreams as a sign that we are approaching an inner integrity and an awareness of the wholeness and harmony of the divine intention. These images represent the inner nucleus of the psyche which transcends the masculine and feminine polarities. Very often the Higher Self appears either as a wise, spiritual, mature person of the same sex, or is symbolised by an androgynous being who is highly evolved and deeply spiritual. The appearance of the Higher Self indicates that we are overcoming the conflict and oppression of polar opposites within. We are effecting an inner marriage of heaven and earth which God displays to perfection and many ancient traditions have sought as their goal.

The message of the *T'ai Chi*, numerology, alchemy, high religions and Jungian psychology is very similar— heaven and earth, spirit and matter, masculine and feminine—are all part of God's plan for creation. Spiritually and psychologically, as well as ecologically and socially, we must recognise the equal and harmonious relationship of these opposites. Failure to do so could lead not only to stagnation but to holocaust.

v. *THE JUDEO-CHRISTIAN TRADITION*

Many of those who have perceived and understood the transcendent wisdom of the union of opposites, are highly critical of the Judeo-Christian tradition because it seems to them to ignore it. Some would be called pagans by many Christians, yet their spiritual sensibilities are outraged by the patriarchal, over-masculine spirit apparent in much Jewish and Christian teaching. The ecclesiastical tendency to portray the 'Father-God' not only as masculine but as wholly male is particularly abhorrent to those who know that the supreme being must transcend sexual characteristics. Many Christians would be very suspicious of the sort of wisdom to be found in the *I Ching* and Jungian psychology etc., yet their own spiritual perceptions are severely limited.

In a recent and much celebrated debate in the Church of Scotland on 'the concept of the Motherhood of God', a specially commissioned study panel roundly condemned those who took God's fatherhood to mean that he is solely masculine. While reaffirming the tradition of calling God 'Father' as commanded by Christ, they also showed that there are biblical precedents for understanding God as 'Mother' as well. For some this seemed to mean that the 'gender' of the Almighty was being questioned. As if he had a gender! As the report said:

> There may be quite innocent, unconscious assumptions on the part of many in the Church that, because we call him Father, and because he has revealed himself in a human being of one sex rather than the other, God has a gender. But we believe that a deliberate affirmation of this view seriously threatens the uniqueness and transcendence of the God to whom all Scriptures witness.[17]

Even the Great Goddess was understood to transcend any one sexual category, and was portrayed as androgynous in order to depict this. Even so-called pagan religions know that no transcendent deity could be limited to one sex, and that the ultimate truth is that gender only points to something higher and infinitely greater, something which knows no bounds of time, space or material existence.

Yahweh cannot be limited by time or space, or any human perceptions of him. He is certainly not androgynous because that is a physical description; and he is spirit. He transcends all such human attempts to depict transcendence, making it clear that his image is only to be found in the creatures man and woman.

Because he was so holy, the ancient Hebrews were forbidden to pronounce the name of Yahweh, only referring to him by the sacred tetragrammaton, YHWH. In some ways this is like the unnamable Tao, yet also very different. Yahweh condemned anthropomorphic images of himself in stone and wood, but did allow himself to be referred to as both father and mother to his people. He was not above using human analogies such as marriage to describe his relations with his people, and in the end he revealed himself in the physical form of the man Jesus. This is the 'folly' of the Christian message, that the great transcendent creator should be made manifest in the *flesh* and should actually die for love of his creation.

God's image was not to be found in stone but in living humanity. It is therefore fitting that the bible should contain images of God which are drawn from the female and motherly realm of experience for, 'We must say of every woman, with no more and no less astonishment and boldness than of a man, that she is "like" God, and that her humanity images and resembles the very Creator of all things'.[18] That creator 'resembles though he far transcends, everything that is best in the female way of being human and the human way of being motherly'.[19]

Despite the considerable threat of the female-dominated religion of the goddess which surrounded the early Hebrews, the bible does contain a surprising number of descriptions which portray the 'feminine' aspects of God and describe God in terms of motherhood. In Psalm 131:2, David tells how he was quieted at God's breast:

> But I have calmed and quieted my soul,
> like a child quieted at its mother's breast;
> like a child that is quieted is my soul.

In Isaiah 49:15, God asks:

> Can a woman forget her sucking child,
> that she should have no compassion
> on the son of her womb?

> Even these may forget,
>> yet I will not forget you.

In Isaiah 42:13–14, Yahweh describes himself as both a man of war and a woman in travail in the space of two verses:

> The Lord goes forth like a mighty man,
> Like a man of war he stirs up his fury;
> he cries out, he shouts aloud,
> he shows himself mighty against his foes.

> For a long time I have held my peace,
> I have kept still and restrained myself;
> now I will cry out like a woman in travail,
> I will gasp and pant.

Both images in these verses are very vivid and active. It is no weak, passive stereotype of woman that he likens himself to, but woman at her very strongest, most desperate and awe-inspiring. Yahweh, using both male and female imagery, described himself in this passage as angry, terrorising, vengeful and destructive. He was the jealous, furious, warrior-god and the agonised mother visiting disaster on his disobedient people, lashing out on mountains, hills, vegetation, rivers, and intransigent humanity (Is. 42:15, 16). But at other times he was merciful, gentle, comforting, pitying and forgiving. His words could be heard just as effectively in the still, small voice. He was 'The Lord, the Lord, a God merciful and gracious, slow to anger, and abounding in steadfast love and faithfulness, keeping steadfast love for thousands, forgiving iniquity and transgression and sin.' (Ex. 34:6). The Lord God was the pitying father and the comforting mother:

> As a father pities his children,
> So the Lord pities those who fear him. (Ps. 103:13).

And,

> As one whom his mother comforts,
> So I will comfort you,
> You shall be comforted in Jerusalem. (Is. 66:13).

Although Yahweh has in many ways been portrayed as the patriarchal God of a patriarchal tribe, he was not limited by a purely masculine range of attributes. He could be both the desperate and the comforting mother, and the jealous and pitying father. To limit God to one single quality, whether male father or female mother is clearly absurd. Something of Yahweh's transcendence over gender comes across in the descriptions of his spirit (*ruach*) and his presence (*shekinah*). Both are feminine words in Hebrew, which highlight the suggestion of the feminine presence of God throughout the bible. It was his spirit (*ruach*) which moved over the face of the waters in Genesis 1; the image is similar to that of a bird hovering over her young in the nest. Although feminine, God's spirit is also very powerful and creative. Even in Genesis 1 the image is that of a bird violently fluttering over her nest. There is a tremendously protective and life-giving vigour in this picture, which is a reminder that without God's spirit there would be no life. Psalm 104 describes the glorious complexities of God's creation, all totally dependent on that 'feminine' spirit for their very existence:

> These all look up to thee,
>   to give them their food in due season.
> When thou givest to them, they gather it up;
>   when thou openest thy hand, they are filled with
>   good things.
>
> When thou hidest thy face, they are dismayed;
>   when thou takest away their breath, they die
>   and return to their dust.

> When thou sendest forth thy Spirit,
>   they are created;
> and thou renewest the face of the ground.
> (Ps. 104:27–30)

As well as expressing the marriage of opposites in an inner way in his character, God also expressed this marriage through his outward relationship to his people and their land. Over the centuries God has become increasingly identified with heaven and with things of the spirit rather than earth and the day-to-day issues of life. This has brought about a divorce between heaven and earth, church and world, spirit and matter which has created a polarisation in many people's thinking about religion. There was no such split in Yahweh's teaching or in the teaching—still less the life—of Christ. So close was Yahweh's relationship with his people, and so much did he want to be one with them that he compared his relationship to a marriage. In the marital imagery Israel becomes the bride of Yahweh! Just as in a human marriage there is a desire to be united with the loved one, a desire for fusion, so God desired not only to love his people, but to be loved by them. In Ezekiel 16, God tells of his love for Jerusalem. She had been like an abandoned child, lying in a field on the point of death before God caught sight of her:

> And when I passed by you, and saw you weltering in your blood, I said to you in your blood, 'Live, and grow up like a plant of the field.' And you grew up and became tall and arrived at full maidenhood. . . .
> When I passed by you again and looked upon you, behold, you were at the age for love; and I spread my skirt over you and covered your nakedness: yea, I plighted my troth to you and

entered into a covenant with you, says the Lord God, and you became mine. (Ezek. 16:6–8)

As we know, Jerusalem proved to be a faithless wife, 'playing the harlot' and going to other lovers such as Ishtar and Baal. But after much cursing and anger, God forgave her. The marriage was restored to both the people and, significantly, the land as well:

> You shall no more be termed Forsaken,
> And your land shall no more be termed Desolate;
> but you shall be called My Delight is in her,
> and your land Married;
> for the Lord delights in you,
> and your land shall be married.
> For as a young man marries a virgin,
> so shall your sons marry you,
> and as the bridegroom rejoices over the bride,
> so shall your God rejoice over you.   (Is. 62:4–5)

The mystical inner reality of God's marriage to his people is foretold alongside the practical outer reality of ecological harmony and prosperity. We know that many disasters came to the people of Israel because of their idolatry and failure to keep God's laws. There were plagues of locusts, pestilence, droughts and famine. The people complained to Jeremiah about these things when he challenged them concerning the worshipping of the Queen of Heaven. They blamed the famine on their failure to be true to Ishtar, but Jeremiah told them this had happened because they were untrue to Yahweh.[20] The reasons may have been hotly disputed, but the ecological disasters were real enough. The people were exiled as much because they exhausted their land's fertility, disobeying God's laws of stewardship, as because of their idolotrous worship. God had laid down very detailed laws in his covenant with the land. The people's failure to keep these laws and make real their own marriage to the land led to exile, for the soil had been exploited and exhausted.

When God and the people, heaven and earth, spirit and matter were one, then there was abundance and prosperity. When they were divorced, there was stagnation, infertility and drought. Just as in Chinese philosophy the yin and yang had to be in a correct balance, and the masculine forces united with the feminine, so God and his people, the King of Heaven and the land of Israel, had to be in the correct relationship according to the law for harmony to prevail. In the words of the *I Ching*, when heaven and earth are one, then there is growth: 'Heaven and earth attract each other, and the transformation and creation of all things is the result. The sages attract the minds of men and universal harmony and peace ensure' (hex. 31). When they are divorced, the growth stops and decay begins: 'Heaven and earth are not in communion. . . . Progressive influences having completed their work, the processes of growth are at an end. Increasing conditions of decay must now be looked for' (hex. 12). Or, in the words of the bible:

> If you walk in my statutes and observe my commandments and do them, then I will give you your rains in their season, and the land shall yield its increase, and the trees of the field shall yield their fruit. . . . And I will give peace in the land, and you shall lie down, and none shall make you afraid; and I will remove evil beasts from the land, and the sword shall not go through your land. . . .
>
> But if you will not hearken to me, and will not do all these commandments, if you spurn my statutes, and if your soul abhors my ordinances, so that you will not do all my commandments, but break my

covenant, I will do this to you: I will appoint over
you sudden terror, consumption, and fever that
waste the eyes and cause life to pine away. And you
shall sow your seed in vain, for your enemies shall
eat it. I will set my face against you, and you shall
be smitten before your enemies . . .

(Lev. 26:3–6, 14–17)

One of the most profound religious expressions of the
marriage of heaven and earth, spirit and matter, in both
an inner and outer way is the symbol of the temple. In
the temple, heaven and earth could come together and
become one. The temple of the Hebrews at Jerusalem
was one of the most symbolic representations of man's
entire religious experience. Its very dimensions and
measurements reflected the coming together of God and
his creation: 'The Temple of Jerusalem was an *imago
mundi* and cosmic centre, a place of communion
between God and Israel; it represented the beginning of
cosmic time and was the dwelling-place or house of God
on earth, a reflection of the Heavenly Tabernacle.'[21]
This temple was divided into two main parts, with an
inner court. According to Josephus, these represented
the three cosmic regions: the lower regions and the sea,
the earth, and heaven. The outer court was the lower
region, the holy place the earth, and the holy of holies,
heaven.

It was the shape of the holy of holies which was most
symbolic. This was God's chamber, and no man or
woman could enter it except the high priest once a year.
God's presence literally filled the holy of holies all the
time—he was constantly with his people and on the land
which he had made. The room was in the form of a cube.
Many symbolists consider the cube to represent the
squaring of the circle, a mathematical feat which the
ancients held to be very potent, for it represented to them

the coming together of heaven and earth. The square with its four sides represented the earth, and the circle the sphere of heaven. The squaring of the circle brought them together in perfect unity—it symbolised the transformation of the sphere of the heavens into the square of the earth and vice-versa. Thus the inner sanctuary of the temple, the sacred holy of holies spoke in its very dimensions of God's unique dwelling with his creation.

There is one book in the Old Testament which has traditionally been described by the rabbis as the 'holy of holies of scripture'. This is the Song of Songs (canticles), a beautifully lyrical love-poem which has been interpreted both literally and allegorically. Taken literally, it is a highly sensual account of the longings of two lovers for each other. Taken allegorically, it is seen as describing the relationship between God and Israel. God is the bridegroom, and Israel the bride. By calling this book the holy of holies the rabbis cast a beautiful and moving light on the meaning of God's dwelling in the temple of Jerusalem and his desire truly to be at one with his people. The temple represented the overcoming of the conflict of opposites and the powerful forces for good issuing from their union.

Jesus Christ played an extraordinarily significant role in this drama of the marriage of heaven and earth, spirit and matter. As both God and man, he held the opposites together in a quite unique way. He was the living mediator between God and his creation. One of the most telling symbols of the meaning of his life came at the moment when he died. Ever since the great temple at Jerusalem had been built, there had been a screen or curtain separating the holy of holies from the holy place. This protected God from the sins of the people and the people from the white heat of his purity. Symbolically, it separated heaven from earth. At the very moment of

Jesus breathing his last on the cross, the curtain was torn in two: the way between heaven and earth was finally opened.

The symbolism of the cross on which Christ died was equally important. It was an ancient symbol dating back long before Christianity, and has been described as the 'cosmic symbol par excellence'. It represented the coming together of opposites, signifying wholeness and restoration. By dying on a cross, Christ made it clear that his message was universal, for the cross appears in civilisations throughout the world. It has great cosmic significance:

> It is a world-centre and therefore a point of communication between heaven and earth and a cosmic axis. . . . The cross represents the Tree of Life and the Tree of Nourishment; it is also a symbol of universal, archetypal man, capable of infinite and harmonious expansion on both the horizontal and vertical planes; the vertical line is the celestial, spiritual and intellectual, positive active and male, while the horizontal is the earthly, rational, passive, and negative and female, the whole cross forming the primordial androgyne. . . . The cross is the figure of man at full stretch; also the descent of spirit into matter.[22]

Christ's death on the cross pointed to his role as mediator between all the opposites. God and humankind, the masculine and the feminine, heaven and earth were all brought together by his life, death and resurrection. Paul made this clear in his letter to the Colossians:

> . . . God wanted all perfection
> to be found in him
> and all things to be reconciled through him and for
> him,

everything in heaven and everything on earth,
when he made peace
by his death on the cross.

(Col. 1:19 and 20, *Jerusalem Bible*)

More specifically in Galatians, Paul reminded his
people that 'There is neither Jew nor Greek, there is
neither slave nor free, there is neither male nor female;
for you are all one in Christ Jesus' (Gal. 3:28). Christ
held in himself a unique combination of spirit and
matter: he was both fully human and fully divine.
Neither element ('nature' in traditional theology) was
more important than the other. His humanity was just as
important to his life as his divinity. He displayed in
himself the perfect balance, the opposites living together
in a wholesome, creative and dynamic union.

He also shared an extraordinary balance of masculine
and feminine qualities in his personality. He was both
creative and receptive, assertive and quiescent, intellectual and intuitive, rational and emotional, for the law yet
disdainful of legalism, analytical and holistic, critical and
compassionate. He was both leader and servant, king
and peasant, victor and vanquished. Jesus Christ was
both the Son of God and a fully human and uncompromisingly male man. He held together in himself the
opposites of yin and yang, masculine and feminine,
spirit and matter, heaven and earth. In this he was the
fulfilment of the alchemists' ideal—the Son of the
Philosopher—the perfectly balanced man, who was in
fact God.

Those who followed the wisdom traditions saw him as
the *logos* or word incarnate. The idea of the *logos* was in
existence long before Christ's birth; for instance, the
philosopher Heraclitus, one of the pioneers of Greek
philosophy who lived around 500 BC, used the word
logos to describe the regulating principle which brought

the conflict of opposites into harmony. He gave this *logos* divine attributes. When John used the term in his gospel, (in English versions calling Jesus 'the Word'), he was aware of the tradition of the *logos*. Rudolf Steiner in his study of the relationship between the mystery traditions and Christianity, explains his understanding of the meaning of the *logos* thus:

> 'The world has come forth from the invisible, inconceivable God. A direct image of this Godhead is the wisdom-filled harmony of the world, out of which material phenomena arise. This wisdom-filled harmony is the spiritual image of the God-head. It is the divine Spirit diffused in the world; cosmic reason, the Logos, the Offspring or Son of God. The Logos is the mediator between the world of the senses and the inconceivable God.'[23]

Jesus was that mediator, that wisdom-filled harmony, but he was no mere concept; he was a man—an historical reality. As Steiner says: 'Something which was a Mystery process in the development of the old wisdom becomes historical fact through Christianity. Thus Christianity became the fulfilment not only of what the Jewish prophets had predicted, but also of what had been pre-formed in the Mysteries. The Cross of Golgotha is the mystery cult of antiquity condensed into a fact. We find the cross first in the ancient world conceptions; at the starting point of Christianity it meets us within a unique event which is to be valid for the whole of humanity.'[24] In John's gospel we read that 'in the beginning was the word, and the word was with God and the word was God.' Christ is the word of God and was with him in the beginning of time. Everything was created by him and for him. In Proverbs 8:1–36 however, we read that wisdom, *sophia*, personified as a prophetess, was also with God in the beginning:

When he established the heavens, I was there,
   when he drew a circle on the face of the deep,
when he made firm the skies above,
   when he established the fountains of the deep,
when he assigned to the sea its limit,
      so that the waters might not transgress his
        command,
when he marked out the foundations of the earth,
then I was beside him, like a little child; [mg.]
and I was daily his delight,
rejoicing before him always,
rejoicing in his inhabited world
   and delighting in the sons of men.

Some Christian traditions, such as the Russian Orthodox, identify this female figure of wisdom with Christ
and the Holy Spirit. It is a central character in much later
Old Testament writings and in the inter-testamental
literature to be found in the apocrypha. This gives a very
moving insight into the beauty of the feminine side of
Christ. He himself high-lighted his 'maternal' qualities
when he said, 'O, Jerusalem, Jerusalem, killing the
prophets and stoning those who are sent to you! How
often would I have gathered your children together as a
hen gathers her brood under her wings' (Matt. 2:37).

In the Wisdom of Solomon, the feminine side of the
creator is even more explicitly and nobly described.
Wisdom here is 'pure emanation of the glory of the
Almighty'; she is strong, intelligent and holy, 'untar-
nished mirror of God's active power, image of his
goodness':

For within her is a spirit intelligent, holy,
unique, manifold, subtle,
active, incisive, unsullied,
lucid, invulnerable, benevolent, sharp,
irresistible, beneficent, loving to man,

steadfast, dependable, unperturbed,
almighty, all-surveying,
penetrating, all-intelligent, pure
and most subtle spirits;
for Wisdom is quicker to move than any motion;
she is so pure, she pervades and permeates all
   things.   (Wisd. 7:22–24)

Let those who dismiss Christianity as too masculine take note of these powerful images of *sophia*, the wisdom of God. Like the early Hebrews, many in the church have been unable to grasp the transcendence of Yahweh and have seen him in their own image rather than recognising the glorious truth that *we* are made in the image of the creator. The bible, however, testifies throughout its pages to the transcendent and infinitely gentle splendour of the creator, a creator who put into the hearts and minds of both women and men the profound desire to see heaven and earth made one.

Chapter Five

The battered bride

As we have discovered, a symbiotic fusion, a marriage of equals between the opposite poles of life, symbolised by heaven and earth and called masculine and feminine, was held to be the ideal pattern for life in a number of different religious and philosophical traditions. Antagonism between the opposites had to be overcome or there would be evil. Domination by one over the other would only break the harmonious balance which was the much desired goal. Everything was understood to contain a spark of the opposite in itself: spirit in matter, matter in spirit; heaven on earth, earth in heaven; masculine in feminine, feminine in masculine. Nothing was exclusively one thing or the other. Tragically however, this picture of mutual love and fusion has proved only to be a metaphysical ideal, not a practical reality. History has shown not a happy marriage of equals, but a battered bride and a searing divorce. Where there should have been complementarity there has been polarisation; where there should have been equality there has been domination; where there should have been harmony there has been disunity.

Our world today is patriarchal—ruled by men and the masculine spirit. As we have seen, the masculine spirit was necessary to enable humanity to understand the mysteries of nature, analyse her secrets and put her gifts to use. Civilisation necessarily requires a certain degree of freedom from the unpredictability of nature, an awareness of individual identity apart from the corporate mass of humanity. These are characteristics of the masculine spirit, which analyses, separates, distinguishes, and brings to consciousness a sense of the self and the other. However, taken too far, a concentration on the divisions between the self and the other, between man and nature can lead to prejudice and exploitation, and can become a *raison d'être* for the categories of oppressor and oppressed. This is what has happened. The predominant spirit of patriarchy—the masculine—has become the oppressor and the feminine has been its victim. Lévi-Strauss wrote: 'Passage from the state of Nature to the state of Culture is marked by man's ability to view biological relations as a series of contrasts; duality, alternation, opposition and symmetry'.[1] The ability to contrast has had its place in the development of human consciousness, but it has gone too far: contrast has become conflict, duality has become dualism, alternation has given way to stagnation, opposition is unnecessarily adversarial, and symmetry has led to suffocating stereotypes.

Nowhere is the fate of the feminine clearer than in the fate of women and nature. It is the traditional view of women that they are 'closer to nature' than men, and both they and nature have been squeezed into a 'feminine' stereotype. This portrays them as submissive, exploitable, inferior to man and the man-made. Women have been regarded as 'unclean'—of the earth, earthy; nature has been called vicious and bloodthirsty—red in tooth and claw. Both have been reduced to matter as opposed to spirit; both have been made into the servant and enemy of man, so people talk of 'the battle of the sexes' and 'man's battle against nature'. What should be seen as dual poles of one nature have been torn apart into a dualistic polarisation of opposites.

The meaning of male and female has been rendered static, stereotyped and finite. Thus women have been identified with the 'negative feminine' qualities of passiveness, intuitiveness, receptivity to emotion, servility and domesticity. The qualities of the feminine have been debased. The qualities of the masculine have been correspondingly elevated, and 'masculine' men are expected to display the 'positive' qualities of assertiveness, leadership, initiative, rationality, self-control and physical strength. The women and men who do not fit these categories are made to feel inferior. Over the centuries, however, it is women who have lost the most, for they have represented all that patriarchy felt obliged to repress and negate. As Simone de Beauvoir wrote,

> '. . . humanity is male and man defines woman not in herself, but as relative to him; she is not regarded as an autonomous being . . . . She is defined and differentiated with reference to man and not he with reference to her; she is the incidental, the inessential as opposed to the essential. He is the Subject, he is the Absolute—she is the Other.'[2]

Of course, as de Beauvoir observed, there are many more who fit the category of unacceptable other. It is not only women who do not conform to the 'norm' for humanity. In the west this category is also filled by blacks, Jews, 'Red' Indians, the disabled, the poor, the Third World, the Russians—the list is endless. Each civilisation has its own outcasts. Racism, élitism, colonialism, sexism, so many divisive 'isms' have been justified by the ruling class's claim that the other is inferior, different, strange, and therefore exploitable.[3]

Women constitute half the human race, and their exclusion from 'normal humanity'—'mankind'—has been a crime of monumental proportions, causing not only deep psychological hurt, but the most desperate physical suffering to women over the centuries. The extraordinary violence shown towards the female species in the following little rhyme from Bulgaria is an indication of women's traditional worthlessness. Because his wife has presented him with nine daughters, and no son, the man promises to reduce her to a blind crippled torso if she has the audacity to be delivered of yet another girl:

> If the tenth, too, is a girlchild,
> I will cut both of your feet off,
> To the knees I'll cut your feet off,
> Both your arms up to the shoulders,
> Both your eyes, too, I will put out,
> Blind and crippled you will be then,
> Pretty little wife, young woman.[4]

The profound hatred of the female displayed in this verse is unfortunately not limited to Bulgaria; it has been world-wide. It has been the practice in a number of cultures, for instance, to leave new-born baby girls on the hillside to die because they were seen to be of no value, only a burden on family finances. Even in China, where the apparently enlightened yin-yang philosophy was so highly developed, an inequitable, male-dominated patriarchal society grew up over the centuries, with extremely repressive attitudes to women which are only now disappearing. This was the view of women in third century China:

> How sad it is to be a woman,
> Nothing on earth is held so cheap,
> Boys stand leaning at the door,
> like Gods fallen out of heaven.
> Their hearts brave the far oceans,
> The wind and dust of a thousand miles.
> No-one is glad when a girl is born:
> By her the family sets no store.[5]

In China, women's feet were bound, to 'improve' the proportions which nature had bestowed and also to keep them under control, securely at home—their husbands' possessions and servants. In the same way, the roots of the bonsai tree were clipped to reduce it to a manageable size—nine inches instead of ninety feet.

Attitudes such as these are not just history, unfortunately. In India today women are still throwing themselves on their husbands' funeral pyres because it has been so deeply ingrained into their minds that without a husband a widow has no right to live. Despite persistent legislation against this practice of *suttee*, it still goes on in remote parts of India where the new message of women's worth has been unable to dislodge the old doctrine of her uselessness. Even more horrific is the continuing practice of bride-burning. There still appear to be great numbers of bride-burnings each year in India, a matter which causes considerable embarrassment to the government. The woman is considered to be so much her husband's property and of such little value in herself that if he decides he has not received a sufficiently large dowry from her father, he will burn her alive in order to remarry and procure a second, hopefully larger amount from his second wife. These examples may be extreme, but the fact that they could happen at all in today's world is an indication of the seriousness of women's problems. There are many horrifyingly inhuman things, such a clitoridectomies and child marriages, done to females in the name of patriarchy which show the end-result of the dispossession of women from their inheritance of equality.[6]

The extent of women's pain, exploitation and suffering throughout the world at the hands of men is still not appreciated by most people. Although in Europe we are very much better off in comparison with our Indian sisters, and many others, nevertheless even here there is evidence of a deep-rooted assumption that a woman is the property of her man, whether father or husband. In the supposedly liberated west it is still taught by many authority figures and governments that a woman's place is only in the home. In Spain the saying goes that a woman's place is at home with her legs broken! This is to keep her the private and manageable property of her husband. Violence against women is still commonplace. The alarmingly high incidence of rape, and the humiliatingly light sentences for the rapist; the widespread, but hidden incestuous molestation; the depersonalising of pornography and the growing numbers of battered wives all testify to a sick society.[7] As the *Scottish Plan of Action* says in its report for the United Nations' Decade for Women:

> Violence against women takes many forms including pornography, rape, incestuous rape and harrassment at work. These are all inextricably linked in a society in which women of all ages are continually degraded, dehumanised and humiliated. Violence against women is not a new phenomenon. It stems from the age old belief that men have a 'right' to control and punish women whether they live with them or not.[8]

Problems such as these have, of course, been the subject of much feminist debate, especially over the past ten or twenty years. At last women are exposing the myths surrounding sexual stereotyping and the degradations which women have received at the hands of men. Patriarchal rule, the rule of the fathers, has been accused and found guilty. The patriarchal religions such as Christianity, Judaism and Islam have been dismissed as being much too male-orientated and exclusive of women. All these have been quite rightly denounced for some outrageous attitudes, and have earned a great deal of the fury and bitterness hurled at them by the Women's Movement. Yet the problem is deeper even than the abuse and exploitation of women. Women have been boxed into a caricature of the feminine, and their fate at the hands of a masculine dominated 'man's world' reflects the fate of the whole of the feminine pole of human experience and of nature.

The association between women and the earth is, as we have seen, an ancient one. The kind, seed-receiving soil has been likened to the kind, seed-receiving womb since earliest times, and both were expected to produce a rich yield for the sower. Such was the attitude of the Earl of Rochester, as illustrated in the following poem to his mistress:

> See the kind seed receiving earth
> To ev'ry grain affords a birth:
> On her no showers unwelcome fall,
> Her willing womb receives them all.
> And shall my Celia be confin'd?
> No, live up to thy mighty mind [*sic*]
> And be the mistress of mankind.[9]

Taunts such as this can grow far more dangerous, however, for what if Celia refuses to yield up her womb for his progeny? Similarly, what happens if the earth refuses to yield and be fertile?

> He breaks the wilderness. He clears the land of trees, brush, weed. The land is brought under his control; he has turned waste into a garden. Into her soil he places his plow. He labors. He plants. He sows. By the sweat of his brow, he makes her yield. She opens her broad lap to him. She smiles on him . . . She is his mother. Her powers are a mystery to him. Silently she works miracles for him. Yet, just as silently, she withholds from him. Without

reason, she refuses to yield. She is fickle. She dries up. She is bitter. She scorns him. He is determined he will master her . . .

He says the land need no longer lie fallow. That what went on in her quietude is no longer a secret, that the ways of the land can be managed . . . In his mind he develops the means to supplant her miracles with his own. In his mind, he no longer relies on her. What he possesses, he says, is his to use and to abandon.[10]

If the traditional connection between Mother Earth and the Earth Mother—nature and women—leads to such patronising and ultimately violent attitudes, then clearly it is a connection which must be resisted. Simone de Beauvoir certainly resisted it. For her it was the mysterious powers associated with women and nature which gave women a mystique and kept them as the Other:

In spite of the fecund powers that pervade her, man remains woman's master as he is the master of the fertile earth; she is fated to be subjected, owned, exploited like the Nature whose magical fertility she embodies. The prestige she enjoys in men's eyes is bestowed by them; they kneel before the Other, they worship the Goddess Mother. But however puissant she may thus appear, it is only through the conceptions of the male mind that she is apprehended as such.[11]

Simone de Beauvoir seems to see nature as in some way opposed to culture and alien to an evolved humanity. Of course, in this case, any identification of women with nature would imply that they are in a less evolved state than men. This is precisely what has been said by scientists, physicians, teachers and spiritual leaders over

107

the centuries. Women have been 'proved' to be intellectually inferior to men—imbecilic, in fact, according to
some!—they have been 'proved' to be more childlike
than men (along with blacks), they have been 'proved' to
be morally irresponsible, spiritually incapable and physically unclean.[12] Freud saw women as in effect second-
rate, 'mutilated men'. His infamous theory of 'penis-
envy' was based on his belief that the majority of
women's problems stem from their awareness of their
inadequacy compared to men. It is no doubt significant
that he also saw women in opposition to civilisation. In
Civilization and its Discontents he wrote:

> Women represent the interests of the family and
> sexual life; the work of civilization has become
> more and more men's business; it confronts them
> with ever harder tasks, compels them to sublima-
> tions of instinct which women are not easily able to
> achieve . . . . What (man) employs for cultural
> purposes he withdraws to a great extent from
> women and his sexual life; his constant association
> with men and his dependence on his relations with
> them even estrange him from his duties as husband
> and father. Woman finds herself thus forced into
> the background by the claims of culture and she
> adopts an inimical attitude towards it.[13]

Culture versus nature = man versus woman. As de
Beauvoir says, 'In woman was to be summed up the
whole of alien Nature.' She sought to liberate women
from this connection, hoping that by freeing women
from 'alien nature' she would also free them from
alienation. Yet there is an even more fundamental
liberation needed before 'women's liberation' can have
any effect: nature must be freed from its category of
'alien'. Freud knew that man's attempts at civilisation,
his repression of his instincts and his relegation of love,

108

had led to an extremely serious imbalance: 'Men have brought their powers of subduing the forces of nature to such a pitch that by using them they could now very easily exterminate one another to the last man.' Women suffer from their association with 'alien nature', but society's alienation from nature affects us all. If the fate of women reflects the fate of the feminine pole, then that pole, and especially Mother Nature, is in a state of rape. As our present ecological crisis shows, unless we overcome our desire to be separated from nature, and also our drive to destroy her, there will be no world in which the newly-liberated women can celebrate their freedom.

The age-old association between women and nature should unite feminism with ecology, not separate them. As historian Carolyn Merchant points out, juxtaposing the goals of these two movements can be extremely creative and productive, suggesting '. . . new values and social structures, based not on the domination of women and nature as resources but on the full expression of both male and female talent and on the maintenance of environmental integrity'.[14] No one can be liberated from nature—we are all part of one creation and depend on our environment for our very existence. But both women and nature must be freed from the shackles of a caricatured feminine stereotype. Nature is no more passive and subservient than are women. Kit Pedler's Gaia was a raging revolutionary. The great Ishtar was ruler of heaven and earth and the whole pantheon. Nature both receives the seed and produces it, both contracts in the autumn and expands in the spring, has both analysable laws and impenetrable mysteries. If we call nature Mother, it should not be to reduce her to the passive feminine stereotype, but to explore the ever-changing complexities of the meaning of mother, which includes the masculine qualities as well. In the same way to call God Father should not reduce him to the 'aggressive masculine' stereotype, but rather expand and elevate our understanding of fatherhood; as Jesus sought so earnestly to do, to his great cost.

In the last chapter we explored some of the Hebrew pictures of God in which he is described in masculine and feminine terms, which reflect both masculine and feminine qualities. He was for instance both the agonised, desperate and violent mother in labour, and the peaceful, comforting mother giving suck. All of life, women and nature included, manifests different aspects of the masculine and feminine at different times. As the Preacher said in Ecclesiastes:

> For everything there is a season,
> and a time for every matter under heaven;
> a time to be born, and a time to die;
> a time to plant, and a time to pluck up what is
> planted;
> a time to kill and a time to heal;
> a time to break down, and a time to build up;
> a time to weep, and a time to laugh;
>
> (Eccles. 3:1–4)

Another way of putting this is that there is a time for yin activity and a time for yang activity. Although this may seem like a blinding insight into the obvious, the fact is that society is so committed to unbalanced yang activity that we are in a profound state of disequilibrium. Something must change. As the Book of Changes, the *I Ching*, tells us, when the yang has reached its climax it must retreat in favour of the yin. The yang has indeed reached its climax, as Austrian physicist Fritjof Capra ably demonstrates in his wide-ranging book *The Turning Point*. His analysis of our contemporary attitudes, as revealed in our social structures, education, medicine, psychology and politics, etc, shows that at the root of many of our modern crises—environmental pollution, economic collapse, world starvation, increased crime and the proliferation of nuclear weapons—lies our obsession with yang rather than yin activity. He lists a few of the traditional qualities associated with yang and yin, which we have already come across:

YIN	YANG
feminine	masculine
contractive	demanding
responsive	aggressive
co-operative	competitive
intuitive	rational
synthesising	analytic

He further observes,

> Looking at this list of opposites, it is easy to see that our society has consistently favored the yang over the yin—rational knowledge over intuitive wisdom, science over religion, competition over co-operation, exploitation of natural resources over conservation, and so on. This emphasis, supported by the patriarchal system and further encouraged by the dominance of sensate culture during the past three centuries, has led to a profound cultural imbalance which lies at the very root of our current crisis—an imbalance in our thoughts and feelings, our values and attitudes, and our social and political structures.[15]

111

One of the causes of our imbalance according to Capra, has been the influence of scientific materialism on society. We pride ourselves on being a 'scientific age', but the scientific paradigms which are being used are often those of an outmoded Newtonian/Cartesian world-view. In this view nature is divided into two unconnected compartments: mind and matter. Matter is seen as inert, dead, unrelated to mind or spirit, and mind is similarly unrelated to matter. It is this reductionist world-view which has dominated scientific thought and the whole of our culture for centuries, but the new physics—of the Quantum Theory and the Theory of Relativity—expose this 'building block' view of nature as fallacious. Mind and matter, time and space, observer and observed, are all seen as part of one cosmic dance of opposites, a seamless web of consciousness. As Capra says, 'In atomic physics, the sharp Cartesian split between mind and matter, between the I and the world, is no longer valid. We can never speak about nature without, at the same time, speaking about ourselves.'[16]

Scientists such as Capra are speaking the same language as the ancient mystics and philosophers, but so far this language seems to be unintelligible to the vast majority of people. Similarly the message of the *T'ai Chi*, that there is nothing in heaven or on earth which is purely spirit or matter, mind or body, that they are complementary, indivisible and equal aspects of the whole; and the message of numerologists that the unbridled masculine energy will end in holocaust; and that of psychological truth concerning the balance of inner opposites, as well as the example of Christ, seem to be incomprehensible to mainstream, modern thinking. It can be no coincidence that so many of the negative effects of the untamed masculine powers represented by the number 666 are evident today. In the past few years we have witnessed the most dreadful 'fantasies of violence, material wealth and power',[17] the tyrannies of self-willed governors and the ultimate holocaust by fire—the nuclear bomb.

Does Christianity have anything to offer this situation? Unfortunately, according to many new thinkers like Capra, who themselves have gone over to the eastern traditions, it not only has few answers, but is itself part of the problem. For instance, Capra believes that:

> The view of man as dominating nature and woman, and the belief in the superior role of the rational mind, have been supported and encouraged by the Judeo-Christian tradition, which adheres to the image of a male god, personification of supreme reason and source of ultimate power, who rules the world from above by imposing his divine law on it. The laws of nature searched for by scientists were seen as a reflection of this divine law, originating in the mind of God.[18]

As we have already seen, the Judeo-Christian God is not in fact a male god, although many Christians seem to think that he is. Beyond gender, he manifests both the masculine and feminine qualities of the women and men whom he made in his image. Nevertheless church tradition has made God seem male, and has built on this 'maleness' to keep women subservient and excluded from spiritual (and other) equalities with men. God has been portrayed as 'safe in his heaven', distant and otiose like the sky gods of Mesopotamia, unconcerned with the matters of earth, uninterested in the more 'feminine' side of his creation and positively hostile to women. It is this spirit/matter divide which has made Christianity the butt of such fierce criticism, particularly from those concerned with environmental and feminist issues. The

113

reasons are plain enough: both women and nature have been relegated to the realm of inferior 'matter', while men have been identified with the 'male' trinity in the distant bliss of heaven.

One of Christianity's most influential critics has been the Professor of Medieval History at the University of California, Los Angeles, Lynn White. White contends that the roots of our present ecological crisis can be found in religious doctrines, and he lays most of the blame on the influence of dualistic, body-alienated Christian teaching. He put forward his views in an article written in 1967, whose impact has been staggering—quite out of proportion to its size. Clearly what he said confirmed the feelings and suspicions of a great number of people, and he is still being widely quoted today. He saw Christianity as one of the world's most anthropocentric and exploitative religions. In his view, 'Christianity, in absolute contrast to ancient paganism and Asia's religions . . . not only established a dualism of man and nature but also insisted that it is God's will that man exploit nature for his proper ends.'[19]

This is a common criticism today and it is voiced by a variety of people. There seems to be little doubt that the predominant emphasis of Christian doctrine has been towards the soul rather than the body, heaven rather than earth. The body and the earth were seen as part of 'fallen nature' and therefore required to be subjugated, enslaved, flagellated and marginalised. Those who have tried to overcome this dualism, or over-emphasis, have been very much in the minority. Augustine wrote that all he was concerned with in his thoughts were 'God and the soul, nothing more, nothing at all.' His example has been diligently followed. Nature as such has seemed to present so many theological problems that it has been left out of most theological thinking; so much so that the great Karl Barth, proving Lynn White's point, suggested that what Christians should discuss is not theology but theo-anthropology![20]

Lynn White's accusations and those of many others are not easy to answer. Anyone who reads the bible will know that it most certainly does not teach that it is God's will that man exploit nature, but that is how it has been interpreted by many Christians, including some of the church's greatest fathers. Dualism, the artificial division between the body and mind, spirit and matter, goes back a long way in Christianity and even longer in philosophy. Plato has often been accused of being the father of a body-denying, hierarchical, spirit-orientated mentality which has dominated church and society in the west. His relegation of physical pleasure and pain to the lower sphere of existence reflects at its most extreme a dualism which disregards and exploits the earth, women and feminine qualities. Because of its influence on ecclesiastical doctrine it has led to the failure of Christianity to offer both women and men the fullness of their humanity as well as their spirituality. The effect of this on men has been bad enough; its effect on women has been catastrophic. Women as representatives of the 'inferior', material earthly side of life have not only been excluded from spiritual equality with men but treated as a sort of deformity and subjected to such violent verbal and physical abuse that it has not infrequently verged on the psychopathic. Rosemary Ruether has stated the problem very plainly:

> Sexism, or the inferiorization of women, is based, symbolically, on misappropriated dualisms. The basic dialectics of human existence: body/soul; carnality/spirituality; Becoming/Being; seeming/Truth; death/life; these dualisms are symbolized in terms of female and male and socially projected as the 'natures' of men and women. The meaning of

115

the 'feminine', then, is modeled, especially in classical ascetic cultures, on the images of the lower self and the world. Autonomous spiritual selfhood is imaged (by men, the cultural creators of this view) as intrinsically 'male' while the 'feminine' becomes the symbol of the repressed, subjugated and dreaded 'abysmal side of man'.[21]

She points out that this dualism has its ultimate expression in the division between God (masculine) and nature (feminine). If we take a look at some of the statements which great religious and philosophical leaders have made about women, and remember that by implication they were saying the same about nature, then we shall understand why both women and the earth are on the point of wreaking their revenge.

Chapter Six

The devil's gateway

Although we live in what many term a post-Christian era, even those in the west who utterly deny any Christian affiliation cannot escape the effects of two thousand years of ecclesiastical influence. The west today reflects Christendom of old and at the heart of many of society's traditions and taboos there often lurk strains of archaic church doctrine and practice. This is particularly true with regard to women. The great Latin Christian father, Tertullian, called women 'the devil's gateway' because of Eve's allurements, and warned that 'God's sentence hangs still over all your sex and his punishment weighs down upon you.'[1] Many women today still feel the weight of this judgment, especially from the churches, but are unaware of the history behind its projection of guilt.

As we have seen, women have long been identified with the earth rather than heaven, with matter rather than spirit, body rather than mind. In many religious traditions this has been painfully explicit through the labelling of women as 'unclean' because of their bodily functions of menstruation and childbirth. (The release of all bodily fluids, from female or male, was considered unclean, of course, but those appertaining to these particular, and purely female, functions were especially so.) The most extraordinary superstitions have surrounded a menstruating woman, for at this time her

117

rhythms appeared to be magical, much closer to the rhythms of nature. Giving birth to a child was also considered unclean, and the patriarchal prejudice comes through clearly when we read in the Old Testament that a woman was considered less unclean if she gave birth to a boy than a girl! She had to stay away from society for fourteen days if her child was female, and only seven if it was male. Woman's nature was considered alien to 'normal' humanity, and as such it has been the subject of much philosophical and religious debate. The writings of the church fathers, reflective as they were of the times and conditioning in which they lived, graphically reveal a deeply dualistic view of soul and body, God and nature, male and female.

Christian teaching has been profoundly influenced by Greek and Latin philosophy, particularly the works of Plato and Aristotle. Indeed, Greek philosophers have been used to answer questions which the scriptures did not cover and in that sense have supplanted the bible on a number of matters. One of the early church's greatest scholars, Jerome, translator of the bible into the *Vulgate,* devoted himself so obsessively to the Greek and Latin classics that he had a vision of Christ, advising him to spend more time on the bible! Jerome's fascination with philosophy was reflected in his extreme asceticism. Martin Luther wrote of Jerome that, 'I know none among the teachers whom I hate like Jerome, for he writes only of fasting, of victual, of virginity, etc. He teaches nothing either of faith, of hope, or of charity, nor of the works of faith.'[2] Much of the blame for our Christian alienation from the body and nature must be laid at the feet of fathers such as Jerome and their philosopher-guides. Plato and Aristotle were completely absorbed into Christian doctrine, inextricably bound up with its history, yet both were deeply misogynist, women representing what they saw as the inferior sphere of existence. People are often ignorant of the extremes to which they and their followers went in their anti-feminist feeling, but it has left a deep mark.

i. *MADE NOT IN GOD'S IMAGE*

Plato believed in the superiority of spirit and mind over the body. He encouraged 'platonic love' rather than physical love, and set his hopes on life after death, despising the material, transient side of earthly existence. Although he appeared at times to give women equality with men, his dualistic thinking always represented them as inferior or as failed men. They had no status as women: '. . . it is natural for women to take part in all occupations as well as men, though in all women will be the weaker partners.'[3] He associated women with the earth, saying that in fertility it was women who learned from nature, not vice-versa. He saw women as at best, a sort of second-rate man, and his most profoundly misogynist comment came in the *Timaeus* where he wrote that: '. . . he who should live his appointed span well should travel back to the abode of his consort star and there spend a happy congenial life; but failing of this, he should change at his second birth into a woman . . .'[4]

In the *Laws* he wrote: 'Woman—left without chastening restraint—is not, as you might fancy, merely half the problem; nay she is a twofold and more than a twofold problem, in proportion as her native disposition is inferior to man's'.[5]

Aristotle categorised women with slaves and non-Greeks and saw them as naturally servile. There was some question about whether in procreation they helped to provide the soul of an embryonic child or only its body. He believed that in a perfect world all humanity would be male, for '. . . the female, in fact, is female on

119

account of inability of a sort . . . and we should look upon the female state as being as it were a deformity . . .'[6] Far from ridiculing such an outrageous statement Aristotle's follower, Thomas Aquinas, restated and expanded it. He was deeply impressed by the works of Aristotle, brought them into his own theology at every opportunity and called him simply, 'the Philosopher'. He too believed that woman was a defective male who only appeared in the world as the result of some dreadful accident to the male seed:

> As regards the particular nature, woman is defective and misbegotten, for the active force in the male seed tends to the production of a perfect likeness in the masculine sex, while the production of woman comes from defect in the active force or from some material indisposition, or even from some external change, such as that of the south wind, which is moist, as the Philosopher observes.[7]

When answering the question 'whether the woman should have been made in the first production of things?', Aquinas gave the reassuring answer that '[God] can direct any evil to a good end'! He had no doubt that it was man who was God's ideal for humanity, '. . . that just as God is the principle of the whole universe, so the first man, in likeness to God, was the principle of the whole human race.'[8] So, according to the great Aristotle and Aquinas, woman was deformed, misbegotten, defective.

The picture of woman as only a second-class human being was of course reinforced by the second account of creation and the fall in Genesis. Paul made much of the chronological sequence of creation in Genesis, using chapters 2 and 3 as the prime reason why a woman should never have authority over a man: 'I permit no woman to teach or to have authority over men; she is to

keep silent. For Adam was formed first, then Eve; and
Adam was not deceived, but the woman was deceived
and became a transgressor' (I Tim. 2:12–14).

It is surprising that Paul should have relied so
exclusively on this account of creation for, as we have
seen, there were two accounts and it was the later one (in
Genesis I) that was generally considered to be more
theological. In it both man and woman were created
simultaneously and equal. Even in the second account it
was not only Eve who became a transgressor; Adam also
sinned and fell. Yet Paul ignored the first account and
interpreted the second as proving woman's inferiority!
Moreover, he went further, implying that woman was
not even in the image of God, again basing his argument
entirely on Genesis 2 and 3: 'A man ought not to cover
his head, since he is the image and glory of God; but
woman is the glory of man. For man was not made from
woman, but woman from man' (I Cor. 11:7–8).

We would do well to note psychologist Erich
Neumann's observation that 'Unnatural symbols and
hostility to the nature symbol—e.g., Eve taken out of
Adam—are characteristic of the patriarchal spirit.'[9]
Paul's loose arguing around this point has done untold
harm to women. Augustine spotted Paul's omission of
any reference to the first account of creation and tried to
reconcile the two, getting himself—and thereby Christian doctrine—into very deep water:

> . . . we must notice how that which the apostle
> says, that not the woman but the man is the image
> of God, is not contrary to that which is written in
> Genesis, 'God created man: in the image of God
> created He him; male and female created He them:
> and He blessed them.' For this text says that human
> nature itself, which is complete in both sexes was
> made in the image of God; and it does not separate

121

the woman from the image of God which it signifies.[10]

All well and good. However, Augustine then goes on to explain when a woman is not in God's image:

> . . . the woman together with her own husband is the image of God, so that the whole substance may be one image; but when she is referred to separately in her quality as help-meet, which regards the woman herself alone, then she is not the image of God; but as regards the man alone, he is the image of God as fully and completely as when woman too is joined with him in one.[11]

Thus Augustine, the greatest of church fathers, spelled out the implications of Paul's teaching: man alone is the glory and image of God; woman is only in his image if she is married! This teaching was crystalised into orthodox Christian doctrine, so that the twelfth century system of church law, the *Decretum* stated categorically: 'The image of God is in man and it is one. Women were drawn from man, who has God's jurisdiction as if he were God's vicar because he has the image of the one God. Therefore, woman is not made in God's image.'[12]

ii. *WOMAN: THE SOUL'S DEATH*

Many things have militated against the equality of men and women, not least the centuries of vitriolic abuse hurled at women in written and oral form. The relegation of women to the inferior, creaturely, abysmal side of life has caused those who felt obliged to reject their own bodies as shameful to reject women as shameful too. The following attitude was very common in Greece, and can still be heard today echoing round the remaining male-monopolised corridors of power.

Protogenes, speaking in Plutarch's *Dialogue on Love* comments,

> I certainly do not give the name 'love' to the feeling one has for women and girls any more than we would say that flies are in love with milk, bees with honey or breeders with the calves and fowl they fatten in the dark. . . . Love inspired by a noble and gifted soul leads to virtue through friendship, but desire felt for a woman leads at best to nothing more than the fleeting enjoyments and pleasures of the body . . . there is only one genuine love, that which boys inspire . . .[13]

For Protogenes, woman was not a noble or gifted soul with whom friendship could be inspiring and uplifting, still less on the basis of virtue! She was only a sexual being and as such unworthy of the superior man's consideration. This view of woman has not only largely excluded them from the decision-making classes and hierarchies of power, but has led to the degradations of sexual abuse such as rape, pornography and prostitution. Such 'schizoid' and non-Christian rejection of the physical creates the paradoxical problem of being out of touch with the health-giving rhythms of the body, while at the same time it frequently leads to over-indulging its desires.

The long tradition behind fear and disgust towards the flesh and its representative, woman, is clearly illustrated in many other writings of the church. One eleventh century French monk felt compelled to compare woman to a dung heap in order to produce the desired attitude of nausea:

> If her bowels and flesh were cut open, you would see what filth is covered by her white skin. If a fine crimson cloth covered a pile of foul dung, would

> anyone be foolish enough to love the dung because of it? . . . There is no plague which a monk should dread more than woman: the soul's death.[14]

Although this was a very extreme way of putting it, it reflects how women were seen as a special threat to the soul, since, according to the church, their very essence was carnal. Many of the early Christians were ascetic and women presented a great temptation to them. Origen was so agonised by this that (following Matt. 5:29f; 18:9) he castrated himself. Even Tertullian, who did marry, wrote letters to his long-suffering wife praising the great virtues of celibacy and asceticism. Heaven and earth were not united in his theology: 'But we read that the *flesh is weak,* and this serves us as an excuse for pampering ourselves in a number of ways. We also read, however, that the *spirit is strong.* . . . The flesh is of the earth, the spirit is of heaven. . . . Should not the things of earth yield to the things of Heaven?'[15]

Jerome neurotically avowed that 'a clean body signifies a dirty mind'. He found all aspects of sexuality abhorrent, encouraged his flock to act against nature if at all possible, and while in the body to live as if out of it. The slimy river-bed of marriage only offered one speck of gold dust to Jerome: 'I praise marriage, I praise wedlock, but I do so because they produce virgins for me, I gather roses from thorns, gold from the earth, the pearl from the shell.'[16]

These attitudes may have been understandable in men who were attempting celibacy, but even within marriage Augustine advised his followers to hate the flesh. A man should love his wife in the same way as Christ commanded him to love his enemy. He wanted there to be no physical pleasure in loving one's wife, and in moments of intimacy he suggested the partners should try to dissociate themselves from their bodies, 'Thus it is

characteristic of a good Christian to love in one woman
the creature of God whom he desires to be transformed
and renewed, but to hate corruptible and mortal
intimacy and copulation—that is, to love the human
being in her, but to hate that which makes her a wife.'[17]

We can only feel pity for both the husband and wife
who tried to follow Augustine's instructions! However,
as he believed that sin originated when a man was
aroused by a woman, this false attitude to marriage was
perhaps logical. Augustine was undoubtedly influenced
by his own sexual adventures before becoming a
Christian, and by the dualistic Manichean heresy to
which he then adhered.

In many religious orders, the celibacy of both monks
and nuns was required, although by no means always
achieved. Women could gain some independence and
even spiritual authority by joining an order and being a
virgin in Christ. Those who won recognition in the eyes
of their male spiritual leaders were given the highest
accolade—they were called 'brother'! But not all women
religious gained this approval. The following 13th
century Premonstratensian charter declared,

> [seeing] that the iniquity of women surpasses all
> iniquities which are in the world, and that there is
> no wrath greater than that of a woman, that the
> poisons of vipers and dragons are healthier and less
> harmful for men than familiarity with women . . .
> we shall receive under no condition any more
> sisters for the increase of our perdition, but rather
> we shall avoid accepting them as if poisonous
> beasts.[18]

It is only when we remember that women symbolised
the body and transfer this vitriol against women to
vitriol against the flesh that views such as these can in
any way be explained. They cannot be excused.

125

Reformers such as Calvin and Luther were deeply critical of some of these worst excesses of the church fathers and their followers. Luther warned his people to '. . . read the Fathers with distinction, considerately. Let us lay them in the gold balance; for the Fathers stumbled oftentimes, and went astray: they mingle in their books many impertinent and monkish things.'[19] Many wise and sensible things were said by them, particularly regarding the importance of married and family life. In this they brought a great deal more respect to woman than previously. There was still a catch however, for according to them a woman's status lay in her role as wife and mother, not as a spiritual equal. She had even less spiritual autonomy than her catholic sisters who had considerable authority as nuns. Heaven and earth were still not one. As Calvin warned: 'If women usurp the right to teach it will be a mingling of heaven and earth.' Such a thing was obviously unthinkable. Martin Luther believed that a woman's physical build equipped her only for bearing, feeding and nursing children, governing their education and running the kitchen. He did not want to see her going off to church on her own, and fasting or praying too frequently. The place of women was in the home, whilst men ran the world: 'The husband rules the house, governs the state politic, conducts wars, defends his own property, cultivates the earth, builds, plants etc. The woman, on the other hand, as a nail driven into the wall, sits at home.'[20]

Sadly, John Knox, one-time colleague of Calvin, though happily married, really vented his spleen against the 'monstrous regiment of women' who had the audacity to teach and even govern men. In a torrent of hysterical outrage Knox accused women of the most exotic crimes which proved them incapable of government:

I might adduce histories, proving some women to have died for sudden joy, some for impatience to have murdered themselves, some to have burned with such inordinate lust, that for the quenching of the same, they have betrayed to strangers their country and city: and some to have been so desirous of dominion, that for the obtaining of the same, they have murdered the children of their own sons . . .[21]

He continued page after page in the same vein, warning that although a man may be blind in many other matters, in this he sees very clearly,

For who can deny but it repugneth to nature, that the blind (i.e. women) shall be appointed to lead and conduct such as do see? That the weak, the sick and impotent persons shall nourish and keep the whole and strong, and finally that the foolish, mad and frenetic shall govern the discreet and give counsel to such as be sober of mind?[22]

It is to Calvin's eternal credit that he was deeply embarrassed by Knox's outburst, and in a letter to Sir William Cecil tried to dissociate himself from Knox whose 'thoughtless arrogance' might have undone all his good work in Geneva and elsewhere, especially England. However, it appears that his own private views about the government of women were not so far removed from Knox's, he was simply more diplomatic about them: 'Two years ago John Knox asked of me, in a private conversation, what I thought about the Government of Women. I candidly replied, that as it was a deviation from the original and proper order of nature, it was to be ranked no less than slavery, among the punishments consequent upon the fall of man.'[23] Calvin admitted that God did occasionally endow women such as Huldah, Deborah and the then Queen of England with special licence to rule, but this was only to teach men a lesson; it was not a natural occurrence.

Attitudes such as these do not merely belong to history. The twentieth century reformed theologian Karl Barth also believed that any attempt to make men and women equal was spiritually misguided. Barth saw man as ruler of woman in the same way as he saw God as ruler of man, masters rulers of slaves, and parents rulers of children: 'Like children in relation to parents, slaves to their masters, the younger to the elder, Christians to the powers that be, women are exhorted and invited to accept their subordination to men not merely as a given fact but in clear self-consciousness, with free will and full responsibility.'[24]

According to Barth, a woman must always be 'B' to man's 'A'. She could not walk side by side with him: she must walk behind: 'Properly speaking, the business of woman, her task and function, is to actualise the fellowship in which man can only precede her, stimulating, leading and inspiring. . . . To wish to replace him in this, or to do it with him would be to wish not to be a woman.'[25] Barth's assumption of woman's subordination to man and the 'given fact' of her inferiority should not of course surprise us, for as we have seen, there have been many arguments over the centuries 'proving' why this is so.[26]

iii. *THE EUROPEAN WITCHCRAFT CRAZE*

One of the most bizarre and shameful episodes in European history was the witchcraft craze, an episode in which both protestants and catholics alike took part and which seemed to be based on a total transference of the sins of the world, the flesh and the devil on to women. This transference began to take place in earnest around the thirteenth century when the traditionally male figure of the devil, prince of the world, became a woman— *Frau Welt*. In literature and sculpture, the worm-eaten, aristocratic male gradually turned into a worm-eaten and beautiful female, often accompanied by that symbol of fleshly lust, the goat. The thinking behind such a transference of devilish evil from a male to a female figure was to have devastating consequences. As historian Eleanor McLaughlin says, *Frau Welt* was 'a public symbol of the high medieval Christian association of the feminine with the evils of sensuality and self-indulgence, for in *Frau Welt* the woman personifies worldly evil, that "materiality" and "fleshiness" which the theological tradition had identified with womankind.'[27] So despised were women during this period that the Latin word for 'woman'—*femina*—was interpreted as meaning 'lacking in faith'. This fanciful play on words reflected a very much more sinister suspicion of women which found practical expression in the atrocities of the witchhunt.

The European witchcraft craze reached its peak in the sixteenth and seventeenth centuries. At the same time as great spiritual strides were being made in the Reformation and Counter-Reformation, and during the supposedly enlightened period of the Renaissance, tens of thousands of mainly harmless women were burned, drowned, beaten and tortured as witches. It is estimated that about one million witches were put to death by both catholics and protestants during the witchhunts—a period which stretched from the later middle ages to the seventeenth century. One Lutheran witch hunter named Benedict Carpazov proudly boasted of having seen to the burning of twenty thousand witches himself.

This was a complex and shocking episode in European history. Many attempts have been made to explain its causes. Some see it as a remnant of Greco-Roman paganism, some as a consequence of the Hundred Years

War and the Black Death; some see witches, along with Jews and other 'heretics', as scapegoats for the misery of the period. But one aspect which has at times been overlooked by traditional historians (although not by feminist ones!) is the fact that most of the victims were women. Not all were women, for it was accepted that the devil could seduce men as well, but the vast majority of alleged witches were female. In the *Malleus Maleficarum*, that great encyclopaedia of demonology, the reasons were most lucidly expounded:

> As for the first question, why a greater number of witches is found in the fragile feminine sex rather than among men. . . . The first reason is, that they are more credulous. . . . The second reason is, that women are naturally more impressionable, and more ready to receive the influence of a disembodied spirit. . . . The third reason is that they have slippery tongues, and are unable to conceal from their fellow women those things which by evil arts they know. . . . they are feebler both in mind and body . . . as regards intellect, or the understanding of spiritual things, they seem to be of a different nature from men;
>
> But the natural reason is that she is more carnal than a man, as is clear from her many carnal abominations. . . . To conclude. All witchcraft comes from carnal lust, which is in women insatiable.[28]

So there we have it: credulity, passiveness, infirmity of body and imbecility of mind apart, the natural and prime reason for women becoming witches was their carnality. Despite the fact that so many of the accused were harmless old women who perhaps knew something about herbalism and natural remedies, the chance to indulge in fleshly lust was considered to be the main attraction of witchcraft. The *Malleus Maleficarum* or *Hammer of the Witches* was an exceedingly popular and highly regarded document. Written by two Dominican priests, Kramer and Sprenger, it was published in 1486, following a papal bull on the same subject in 1484. Between then and 1520, it went through fourteen editions and lay on the benches of judges and magistrates of both catholic and protestant faiths during the period of the craze. Amazingly, the high acclaim which this document received has not been limited to that time alone. Its modern translator, the Reverend Montague Summers admitted to being deeply impressed by it. As he commented in his introduction of 1946: 'It is not too much to say that the Malleus Maleficarum is among the most important, wisest, and weightiest books of the world. . . . What is most surprising is the modernity of the book. There is hardly a problem, a complex, a difficulty, which they have not foreseen and discussed, and resolved.'[29]

Presumably, Montague Summers agreed with Sprenger and Kramer that woman is 'but a foe to friendship, an inescapable punishment, a necessary evil . . . an evil of nature.' He certainly did not seem to be put out by this as he eulogised the work for its wisdom and modernity, describing it as being 'argued with unflinching logic, and judged with scrupulous impartiality.' For those who are inclined to dismiss the anti-feminist feelings described in this chapter as ancient idiocies, let Montague Summers be a warning. Such feelings are still abroad today and still deprive women of their personhood.

In his controversial analysis of the European witch-craze, the celebrated historian Hugh Trevor-Roper attributed much of the blame to a dualistic doctrine in the church. According to him, the inevitable corollary of Thomas Aquinas's exhaustive systematisation of God's

131

kingdom, his *Summa Theologica,* was a systematisation of the devil's kingdom, the *Malleus Maleficarum.* Aristotelian cosmology was behind both systems and as Trevor-Roper says, 'St. Thomas Aquinas, the guarantor of the one was the guarantor of the other.'[30] The simplistic division of life into light and darkness, good and evil, easily became a polarisation between 'those for us' and those 'against us'. According to this thinking, heretics were witches and witches were heretics. Thus Jews, Albigensians, Moors, all those who did not conform to the 'norm', were heretics and witches, scapegoats for all evils. Catholics were witches to protestants and protestants were witches to catholics. The religious wars of this period helped to fan the fires of the witch-pyres just as religious bigotry fans the fires of terrorism in Northern Ireland today.

Trevor-Roper very harshly condemns both Augustine and Thomas Aquinas as the founders of demonology and fathers of the witch-craze. Aquinas he accuses of being tainted by Aristotelian cosmology and Augustine by Manichean heresy. It was the influence of their theology with its concentration on the divisions of life which, according to Trevor-Roper, led to the atrocities of self-righteousness, bigotry and cruelty during the craze. It is highly significant (although like most historians Trevor-Roper does not comment on it), that it was mainly women who represented darkness, evil, supernatural wickedness, fleshly lust and who were burnt at the stake. As Kramer and Sprenger said, they were 'an evil of nature'. Perhaps they represented 'evil nature'? The church fathers including Aquinas and Augustine taught much that was deeply spiritual and wise: they also taught much that was body-alienated and foolish. They and the Greek philosophers have left a legacy of dualism which still haunts the Christian church.

iv. *THE SCHIZOID HERESY*

Augustine wrote that a woman was in God's image in her body only if she was married. A single man was in God's image in both mind and body whether married or not. Although Genesis I categorically states that Elohim made humanity in the image of the transcendent deity—male and female, the church has been unable to accept the radical equality this has granted to women. Our patriarchal ecclesiastics have portrayed God not only as masculine, but male. In the Roman Catholic Church the priest is considered to be God's unique representative, his vicar on earth. A masculine God can only be represented by a man, so the argument goes. The man is the bridegroom; the woman represents the subservient earthly bride, the church of God. While God is confined to masculine imagery alone, the ordination of women to the catholic priesthood will be impossible. As early as 1963, Pope John XXIII warned that women will no longer tolerate being refused their rights as human beings:

> Since women are becoming ever more conscious of their human dignity, they will not tolerate being treated as mere material instruments, but demand rights befitting a human person both in domestic and public life . . . Human beings have the right to choose freely the state of life which they prefer, and therefore the right to follow a vocation to the priesthood or religious life. (*Pacem in Terris*, 1963)

Unfortunately, the situation has become less, rather than more, tolerable for Catholic women under the present Pope.

The Church of England is also full of anomalies on this issue. Despite a decision of the 1975 Synod which ruled that there is no fundamental theological objection

133

to the ordination of women, the church has consistently refused to grant them that right. In an historic vote in 1978, the motion to ordain women was defeated by the Church of England clergy who voted overwhelmingly against the motion, although the majority of bishops and laity were in favour. Many women were devastated. As Una Kroll cried from the spectators' gallery, 'We asked for bread and you gave us a stone!' Some Anglican priests seem to have a profound and irrational fear of women in their ranks. In 1973 the Bishop of Exeter made the extraordinarily abusive comment that the admission of women to the priesthood would herald a subtle shift towards the old pagan religions, and would threaten the church's witness 'in a sex-obsessed culture.'[31] Such utter nonsense is not only ignorant but deeply insulting, especially to those ordained women of other denominations who have not indulged in the orgiastic rites of the old pagan religions! There is something seriously amiss in a church where such sentiments can be given voice. (Happily, this state of affairs has been changed in the historic decision of the Synod of the Church of England which, in November 1984, voted in favour of women priests.)

Although many presbyterian churches do allow women into the ministry, many of the women themselves feel regarded as surrogate men. The emphasis is still very much on masculine dominated structures, a masculine God, leaving to women the serving roles. Equality in theory may have been given, but its reality is still far off. This is more or less true of the whole range of activities open to women. In our masculine, 'yang' dominated society, with its traditionally male-monopolised churches, the feminine, women themselves, nature, the earth, the intuitive and the holistic view of life have been relegated to the 'repressed, subjugated and dreaded "abysmal side of man".'[32]

cerned about the damage done by what he calls 'schizoid intellectual theologians'—the men (and women) who have tried to escape the pain and perplexities of bodily reality by splitting off into spiritual and mental abstractions. As he says,

> . . . schizoid deviations . . . have distorted the Church's life, taken the common touch from her message, seduced her theologians, sold her leadership into bondage of academic and social 'aristocracies', dragged her training from the streets into the schools, substituted manners for morals, neglected her historic mission, stolen a real earthly future from her hope, gone back on the birthright of her women, exalted knowledge above love and thought above action.[35]

These are serious charges. All the more so because the church's mistakes inevitably affect society. Our schizoid world is the outcome of centuries of unbalanced thinking and psychological disorders among some of our most highly respected theologians and philosophers. As Lake has said, 'So much that has on this pretext joined the Church's grand parade should now be identified as pathology.' Yet the Christian message is one of love and acceptance, not pathological fear and hatred. There should be neither Jew nor Greek, slave nor free, male nor female, for we are all one in Christ. Our future depends on identifying the mistakes of the past and finding a new holistic paradigm. Just as the Great Mother Gaia will no longer passively suffer the damage done to her, nor will women any more be the subservient recipients of men's projected guilt. The way forward is not the way of stultifying reductionist polarisation, but the way of unity, wholeness and mature love.

137

Chapter Seven

Archaic fears

> If the relationship between two people can be made creative, fulfilling, and free of fear, then it follows that this can work for two relationships, or three or one hundred or, we are convinced, for relationships that affect entire social groups, even nations. The problems of the world—and they are chronicled daily in the headlines of violence and despair—essentially are the problems of individuals. If individuals can change, the course of the world can change.[1]
>
> Thomas A Harris

The most important biblical commandment is that we should love God with all our hearts, minds, souls and strength, and our neighbours as ourselves. However, over the centuries many church leaders have tragically failed not only to love others, especially women, but even to love themselves. Their fear of women seems to have reflected a fear of their own bodies, just as the fear of nature as 'red in tooth and claw' reflects the anxiety that our own natures might also be vicious and wild if given half a chance! An over-emphasis on sin and the need for redemption has obscured the glorious life-affirming truth that God made *everything* and it was good.

Fear is the great destroyer of life. It is fear that paralyses the schizoid child; denies women their birthright of equality; sets up impenetrable barriers against nature; and it is fear that brings enmity between people and war between nations. Fear of failure, exposure, ridicule, rejection, hurt, death—so many named and unnamed fears inhibit life and growth. We are now in the age of the Cold War—the age of a chilling frozen fear which barricades itself in with neurotic intensity and self-destructive determination. As psychologist Thomas Harris has emphasised, the problems of the world are essentially the problems of the individual. Just as no individual relationship can be healthy if it is full of fear, neither can the state of the world be healthy while the super-powers and smaller nations are so intensely afraid of each other. Similarly the state and growth of the church cannot be healthy so long as there is a dread and fear of women and the feminine.

In his highly popular book, *I'm OK—You're OK,* Thomas Harris puts forward a simple and widely accessible interpretation of the psychological method invented by Dr Eric Berne, called Transactional Analysis, (T.A.). Through this Berne created a simple, clear, non-technical language with which to tackle psychological problems—both individual and social. His vocabulary made it possible for two people to talk about behaviour meaningfully, without a full training in psychoanalysis. Harris's book made Berne's method even more understandable, and brought psychological awareness to hundreds of thousands of people. His great message was that people *can* change. We can take control of our lives by becoming aware of what psychological 'games' we play, what roles we adopt, and what negative influences from the past hinder our present. He also helped to explain why certain social groups, even nations, behave as they do, and therefore offers a tool with which to interpret history. Very helpful points have emerged from its application to some of the issues in this study. We take first a brief look at the T.A. method.

i. *I'M OK—YOU'RE OK*

Transactional Analysis offers three categories—Parent, Adult and Child—with which to interpret actions and reactions. These are not people; they are roles within each individual (almost differing aspects of the alter ego), which he or she adopts at any given moment, thus the Parent-role, the Adult-role and the Child-role. Continual observation and experiments have revealed that these three states of mind exist in everybody, imprinted on our brains and in our psyches. We each have within us the same person we were when we were very young, we each have the recorded messages of our parents still ringing in our ears; and we each have the potential to assess and transcend the influence of this Child and Parent within. We assess these with our Adult response.

According to Berne, the experiences of the first five years are the most crucial, leaving their mark (both conscious and unconscious) on the character, beliefs and capabilities of each individual. Miseries of frustration and hurt in childhood can stunt our growth and interfere with adult relationships. The parental commands of years ago can still have the power to move us, and can sound like the voice of inviolable authority. Those early experiences mould our pattern of growth, 'play old tapes', and affect our transactions with others.

In a sense both the Child and Parent rely on archaic material, accumulated during the impressionable first five years, and not necessarily relevant to the contemporary situation. It is the task of the objective Adult to assess the truth of the feelings of the Child and the criticisms of the Parent. The Adult capacity apparently develops in any normal infant at around ten months.

Within each individual these three states of mind coexist, and they interact in different ways according to the situation or person. The Child can give us a sense of play and fun, as well as emotional vulnerability and dependency. The Parent can give us wise, important advice as well as archaic admonitions. However, whether we adjust in a mature way to these inner messages is dependent on what Harris calls our life-position. He defines four life-positions which are so simple that they provide an invaluable guide to many problems. These are:

I'M NOT OK—YOU'RE OK
I'M NOT OK—YOU'RE NOT OK
I'M OK—YOU'RE NOT OK
I'M OK—YOU'RE OK

The first position is perfectly normal, although a position of inferiority. According to Harris every young child, however cared for and loved, feels inferior. Being tiny, dependent and ignorant, compared with the huge, omniscient parents, the child feels NOT OK, but believes that the parents and everyone else are OK in comparison. This attitude can continue right into adulthood, but it is not conducive to healthy, loving relationships. The Child within must be taught to love him or herself, as the parents have loved it in childhood.

However, if its parents did not love it, or were undemonstrative and distant, the child may have come to the conclusion that they too were NOT OK, giving it the life-position I'M NOT OK—YOU'RE NOT OK. This attitude can lead to depression, and in some cases even suicide in later years.

If the child is actually abused—physically or emotionally battered—then he or she may be unable to face reality, and withdraw from social contact, retreating into a personal fantasy world. The deeply distressed and

dangerous life-position caused by this is I'M OK—
YOU'RE NOT OK. It can turn into an attitude of
cruelty, violence, intolerance and self-righteousness. At
its worst it leads to the position of the criminal
psychopath who feels no remorse.

The first three life-positions are fragmented and full of
fear. For life to become creative, happy and fulfilled
they must be transformed into the liberating life-
position: I'M OK—YOU'RE OK. This is the joyful
attitude of self-acceptance and acceptance of others. It
can be found through our objective Adult response
which assesses the 'old tapes' of the past, the fear and
pain of the child and the strength of the parents'
convictions. It gives the authority to rise above the
bondage of old hurts, to gain control of its feelings, to
stop projecting its problems on others and so achieve the
life-affirming state of mind which declares I'M OK and
YOU'RE OK. This is a statement of love—not a
masochistic, neurotic self-denial, but an over-flowing
self-giving which encompasses everyone. For those who
achieve this position of maturity, every single person has
value, including themselves; no person can be devalued,
no person is NOT OK, Other, outcast or inferior. In
this attitude of love and acceptance we can say:

> I am a person. You are a person. Without you I am
> not a person, for only through you is language
> made possible and only through language is
> thought made possible, and only through thought
> is humanness made possible. You have made me
> important. Therefore, I am important and you are
> important. If I devalue you, I devalue myself.[2]

This is the meaning of loving others as we love
ourselves; it is the reality of redemption, reconciliation
and enlightenment—a theme which is central to many
great world religions. It is the returning of people to

their rightful place of full personhood. It is the very essence of God's command that we love him first, and others as ourselves. The experience of Christianity leads to this realisation: I'M OK—YOU'RE OK.

In many ways the Christian church has shown great love and care towards the dispossessed NOT OK. It was the Christian impulse which led, for instance, to the abolition of the slave trade, to penal reform in the 19th century, to voluntary social aid and care for the poor. The innumerable homes, hospitals, schools and other pastoral and caring services pay tribute to Christian compassion as do many missionary activities overseas. Unconditional love is a very hard concept for people to grasp, especially if they themselves did not experience being fully loved or accepted by parents, teachers or friends. However, in many other areas the church has instigated and perpetuated a deeply self-righteous and condemning attitude of YOU'RE NOT OK towards those who do not conform to its theological ideal, and therefore pose a threat. The sort of universal love which Christ manifested does not build up dogmas, creeds or constitutions which have to be signed, power structures which have to be deferred to, labels which have to be displayed. Truly unconditional love does none of these things. It accepts people where they are with all their failures, fears and peculiarities. This was the difference that Jesus made.

The church would have been a very different place if it had heard and obeyed his radical message of self-acceptance and acceptance of the other. Anyone who reads the bible cannot fail to be struck by its constant exhortations to love others as oneself. Yet the history of Christianity is anything but a story of love. All too often it is a story of bloody battles, petty rivalries, persecutions, oppressions and wars. The superior, violent intolerance of the I'M OK—YOU'RE NOT OK position has often been more characteristic of the church than the joyful openness of I'M OK—YOU'RE OK. As Harris says,

> The non-Adult transmission of Christian doctrine has been the greatest enemy of the Christian message of grace. . . . The I'M OK—YOU'RE OK message has been twisted again and again to a WE'RE OK—YOU'RE NOT OK position under which sanction Jews have been persecuted, racial bigotry has been established as moral *and* legal, repeated religious wars have been fought, witches have been burned, and heretics have been murdered.[3]

Christian intolerance extends over a very wide area, but as we have seen, it was that fallen woman Eve who received the church's emphatic projection of NOT OK. Applying the insights of T.A. to her and her female representatives can prove to be a very enlightening exercise. Tradition has it that it was as a result of Eve's sin and seduction that evil itself came into the world. Eve has been called the 'devil's gateway', and women have inherited that stigma and guilt. Jesus did not see women in this light. He was startlingly revolutionary in his acceptance of and love for them. Against the traditions of his day, his attitude to women was I'M OK—YOU'RE OK. In his time Jewish men could not speak to a woman publicly, even if she was his wife or daughter. No woman could enter into a theological discussion with a man, nor could she be taught by a man, especially a rabbi. A woman's testimony was considered to be of no worth. So inferior was woman's status, that Jewish men were taught to pray: 'Blessed art Thou, Lord our God, King of the Universe, who made me not a woman.'

In contrast to this, Jesus' attitude to women was

unprecedentedly loving and respectful, accepting their value as equal to that of men. He often spoke to women in public, even the woman taken in adultery whom he addressed and forgave; women were among his closest friends and followers. Jesus openly engaged the woman of Samaria in a theological discussion, yet on at least three counts she was totally NOT OK to her society. She was a woman, she was a Samaritan, and she had had five husbands and was even then living with another man who was not her husband. For this reason she was forced to fetch water in the heat of the day, thus avoiding the respectable women who were at home. Yet the rabbi Jesus treated her with great respect and understanding, offering her acceptance.

Jesus gently chided his friend's sister Martha who became so critical of her sister Mary for departing from the woman's role of cook, and sitting at Jesus' feet to be taught. He told Martha that far from deserving censure, Mary had chosen 'the better part'. His sympathy for the plight of women was movingly illustrated in his treatment of the haemorrhaging woman. She was so determined to be healed and so sure Jesus had the power to do it, that she touched the hem of his cloak, although her condition had rendered her permanently unclean. Instead of allowing her to be quietly healed and creep away, Jesus insisted on publicly identifying her, and talked to her—an act of total affirmation.

At the most vital moments in his life and ministry, it was women who supported Jesus. Not only did they support him through his public life, but they were with him when he died, and were the first to see him alive again. He first appeared to Mary when he rose from the dead and it was *her* testimony that the other disciples accepted as truth. There are many more instances of Jesus' love towards the socially unacceptable women which proclaimed his message, 'I'M OK—YOU'RE

OK'. How sad it is that over the years the church has proved so unwilling to follow his example! It has been greatly impoverished as a result and has caused considerable anguish to others.

ii. *THE ENDURING SHADOW OF THE GODDESS*

In the language of TA, the church's attitude to women has been WE'RE OK—YOU'RE NOT OK. However, as Harris shows, despite its extreme self-righteousness, this position is one of deep distress, caused by an early and traumatic experience. What was it that created this neurosis in the church?

As we saw in chapter two, the early centuries in the history of the Hebrew people were haunted by terrible battles between Yahweh and Ishtar, the King of Kings and the Queen of Heaven. So bloody was the fight, and so intransigent were the Hebrews in their devotion to the goddess, that exile from their beloved land was the only punishment which Yahweh finally considered dire enough to teach them their lesson. After that first exile, the Jews were never the same again. That dreadful experience brought on by the worship of the goddess, and her followers' behaviour, was probably one of the most crucial events which led to the church's later fear and dread of women. It was foreign women who led their husbands astray and it was a female goddess who threatened and so angered Yahweh.

For the Jews, the exile was a catastrophe. The battering which reaction to the goddess inflicted on their fortunes left an indelible mark. As Rosemary Ruether suggests the struggle between Yahwism and the goddess religion was 'one of the most important influences shaping Old Testament religion'.[4] It may have led to the rejection of feminine descriptions of God and the rejection of female religious leaders. In other words, it led to a masculinising of a supposedly transcendent God and the domination of men in an increasingly patriarchal religion.

The Jews returned chastened from exile. They had learned their lesson regarding idolatry, and the seductive goddess had been rooted out. However, as is the way with such intense episodes, it was not forgotten. Indeed, despite the fact that the goddess religion was at its peak so long ago, and although the battles between her and Yahweh took place between two and three thousand years ago, she still casts a shadow over religion today, as she did in fact over the exiles of the restoration, hence the savagery of Ezra's campaigns (Ez. 10:9–12).

For millenia she has wielded an archaic power over the minds and traditions of the Hebrew people and their legatees, the Christians. Just as grown people can have an archaic reaction to something which reminds them of their early experiences as a child, so it seems that many religions have had an archaic reaction to the ancient power of the goddess long after she had been defeated by the patriarchal male gods.

Clear evidence of the Jews' archaic dread of the goddess can be found in a traditional folk-tale which was woven around the woman who was made in God's image in Genesis 1. As we have seen, that account of creation was written by the priests after the exile and was purified from its former polytheistic influences. The equal status of woman and man in this account was in marked contrast to the earlier story of Adam and Eve. However, it appears that the freedom and independence of the woman in Genesis 1 proved too radical for those Jews who wanted to keep women subservient and who still remembered the stories of the goddess. So they made her into a separate woman.

Jewish tradition as found in the *Talmud*, separated the

two stories of creation, and built an entire myth around the woman of Genesis 1, dissociating her from Eve. Just as Augustine went through theological somersaults to explain away the differences between Genesis 1 and 2, so the Jews fabricated a legend to do the same. According to this legend, the first man and woman were Adam and Lilith. Lilith was Adam's wife: fierce and independent. She did not appreciate Adam's attempts to make her subservient, nor his easy assumption of superiority. So, after a time, she took off, leaving God and Adam to find a replacement. This they did, calling her Eve. But it was made very clear to Eve that she was not Adam's equal, only his helper.

Meanwhile, Lilith (whose name means 'screech-owl'!) was turned into a blood-sucking monster of the night who haunted the deserts, attacked women in childbirth and had a particular penchant for murdering young boys. Behind the story of Eve we find the goddess lurking; it would appear that she also lurks behind the story of Lilith. Robert Graves has observed that very often the demons and bogeys of one religion are in fact the reduced gods and priests of another since superceded.[5] He sees the screech-owl Lilith as a remnant of the ancient worship of the goddess of wisdom, observing that its symbol the owl '. . . occurs on the coins of Athens as the symbol of Athene, the Goddess of Wisdom . . . the same owl that gave its name to Adam's first wife Lilith . . .'[6] The Jews could not forget the ancient threat of the goddess with her priestesses and devotees. The OK woman of Genesis 1, like Eve, was made NOT OK in order to keep women in their place. Even the purged priestly account of creation, which had been so carefully cleared of references to other deities, was expanded in popular thought to include a warning of the horrors of the blood-sucking goddess and the pride of women.

148

iii. *CHRISTIAN CONSEQUENCES*

Jewish history is of fundamental importance to the Christian tradition. The Old Testament is the story of the Jews, as well as being the word of God. Since Christianity is based on the bible—Old and New Testaments—every episode is seen as having some relevance today. However, it has to be seen in its historical context. The Jews' battle with Ishtar happened between two thousand and four thousand years ago, yet for some it is as if it were yesterday. The same intolerant and fearful attitude of I'M OK—YOU'RE NOT OK is held against the feminine, in an absurd and anachronistic fashion. For instance, in a study of biblical vocabulary one scholar felt obliged to observe, in an otherwise objective article, that 'the queen of heaven . . . as emerges so clearly from such passages as Jer. 7:16–20 and 44:15–30, has ever exerted a great power to seduce the feminine temperament'.[7] What exactly he meant by this statement is a mystery, but his scorn of the credulous 'feminine temperament' is very evident.

The polemics continue yet. As we saw, one Church of England bishop feared that the introduction of priestesses would be a return to 'sex-obsessed' nature religions. This was an extraordinary remark. C S Lewis also feared any hint of the femininity of God or the introduction of women into the ministry, saying that the religions which had goddesses and priestesses were quite different from Christianity.[8] On the issues of using feminine symbols for God and the introduction of ordained women, there have been some outrageous comments made by otherwise thoughtful people. The terms 'goddess' and 'priestess' apparently possess strongly emotive power, but it is a power that is out-dated, and any fear of it is archaic, irrelevant and positively damaging both to those who set up siege against the feminine and those who are

Freeing the Feminine

consequently excluded. We must examine ourselves for
signs of the distressed but destructive attitude of I'M
OK—YOU'RE NOT OK towards the feminine and
women. One of the most distressed and indeed distres-
sing examples of this attitude was the Church of
Scotland's reaction to its own commissioned report on
the theological implications of the concept of the
Motherhood of God. This report was scholarly, well-
balanced and not in the least revolutionary, yet it was
vilified by many in the church, including a great number
of ministers, simply because it did not stop at reaffirming the Fatherhood of God, but went on to demonstrate that the bible itself sanctions female and motherly
images of God. We have looked at some of these
pictures, which of course are so few because of the
ever-present threat of the nature religions and their
powerful goddesses. However, the impact of the fertility
rites of surrounding countries also had the effect of
making the writers of the Old Testament very careful
about using the term father to describe God, for the
male deities were just as active in cultic marriages as the
goddesses. We are not afraid of calling God father
today, because Jesus himself called God his father and
commanded us to do the same. He did not mean to limit
God in any way, but rather to expand our awareness of
the intimate love God has for each of us. It was highly
revolutionary in his day, considered in fact to be nothing
less than blasphemous by the religious leaders.

The bible contains several descriptions of God using
female and motherly terms, and some earlier church
traditions also seemed to be less reticent about using this
imagery than we are today. One seventh-century church
council affirmed both the fatherly and motherly qualities
of God by asserting paradoxically that the Son was born
'from the womb of the Father'. Similarly, Anselm asked
'And you, Jesus, are you not also a mother?', and

declared 'So you, Lord God, are the great mother'.

Julian of Norwich is perhaps the most celebrated of those who saw God as mother. With great eloquence and poetry she described Jesus Christ as 'our true Mother' and poignantly observed that 'A Mother may feed a child with her own milk, but our precious Mother, Jesus, feeds us with Himself, courteously and tenderly, with the blessed Sacrament, the blessed food of life.'[9]

Despite these inspiring and elevated insights into the profound love which God has for us, a love which can be compared to, though it far transcends, the love of a mother at its best, there is still an overwhelming fear on the part of many in the Christian church today of releasing the more feminine aspects of our creator into our consciousness. This must be due partly to growing fear of feminist infiltration, as well as a fear of women themselves. As one journalist put it in the controversy surrounding the Church of Scotland debate: 'The intrusion of feminists is getting a bit much. It was bad enough that they wanted to be elders and even ministers, but now they want to go right to the top and take over God.'[10] Or as one woman complained: 'Many of us feel that "sexism" has really gone too far, when the gender of the Almighty is being questioned!'[11]

Does God have a gender? Perhaps this woman had it on the same authority as the journalist who declared: 'God IS a man. My Sunday-school teacher said so.'[12] According to one antagonist, sanctioning even the 'limited use of feminine gender in relation to God' would 'give a foothold to more radical feminist elements who seek to justify a more dominant feminine presence in the Church, which is not endorsed or supported by the whole tenor of scripture'.[13]

What do these people have against the feminine? For

some, no doubt, their resistance to thinking of God as mother is because of an unconscious (or perhaps conscious!) acceptance of the traditional demeaning of women and their association with uncleanness. To call God mother would be inconceivable to those who hold this view, for it would identify him too closely with the unclean, spiritually NOT OK human mother. But for many others, the idea of God as mother is offensive explicitly because it makes him sound like the Goddess. Clearly the church has not recovered from the effect of the sufferings endured by the Jews because of their persistent attachments to the Goddess over three thousand years ago. The very word 'goddess' seems to conjure up some picture of orgiastic nature rites and female domination. No one ever suggested that the creator should be made into a pagan goddess, yet again and again the Great Goddess comes into the debate. In the Church of Scotland's report, repeated reference is made to the fact that the panel is not trying to turn the God of Jesus Christ into a pagan goddess or female deity. There is a horror of this in many people's minds, but they still accept him as a male deity. Is that inherent chauvinism any less pagan? At the end of the report it is re-affirmed that the panel is not flirting with neo-paganism but is examining the question of the 'mother-hood of God' without reference to the unbiblical neo-pagan goddess religion. The very fact that they bring the goddess into their report is significant. She undoubtedly was very powerful three thousand years ago. As Visser't Hooft says in his book, *The Fatherhood of God in an Age of Emancipation*, 'In the Apostolic age, mother goddesses with their fertility cult were still a force to be reckoned with.'[14] But is the fertility cult *still* a cult to be reckoned with? Is not our fear of the pagan goddess now anachronistic? Apparently not, judging by the frequent references to her.

In a letter to *The Scotsman,* following the public prayer of the president of the Woman's Guild addressing God as 'Dear Mother God'—a prayer which started the controversy—one minister wrote, 'Apropos of Mistress [*sic*] Hepburn's ideas regarding the sex of God . . . It was tried of old. Demeter, the Earth Goddess, was I believe, the Great Mother. She was, however, in spite of the projection upon the Godhead of human ideas of procreation, conception and childbirth, found to be inadequate for reasons which are impossible to define with any accuracy now.'[15] All 'Mistress' Hepburn had done was to address a prayer to God as Mother and suddenly there was the Goddess! Like many others, unfortunately, but surprisingly for a minister, the correspondent seemed to lack any concept of the transcendence of the Almighty over gender. He was afraid that the Woman's Guild president was attempting to dispense with the idea of God as male, as indeed she was, and warned that '. . . in abandoning the maleness of God we may be taking the first step down the path of, not a new theology, but of a neopolytheism. The next step will be to divide God up into various manifestations, sexually different from one another to satisfy the feeling of both sexes.'

It is not the president but the minister and those like him who insist on God's maleness, who introduce polytheism, as the report made abundantly clear. The highly theological writers of Genesis 1 used 'Elohim' to convey his oneness and transcendence; those who try to make him uncompromisingly masculine reduce him to something akin to an Iron Age Marduk.

Just as men and women have been pushed into severely restricting stereotypes of behaviour and character, so many people wish to keep their creator confined to a male personality and a masculine role. They fear that to do otherwise would impair his image and recreate

153

the battle between the Great Father God and the Mother Goddess. But our world is very different from that of three thousand years ago. We must not allow the fearful Child within to overwhelm the Adult with irrational fears of the historical goddess, nor must we tolerate the unanalysed taboos of our inner critical Parent who blindly insists on following convention and keeping the peace.

Understandably, for those who do not understand the ancient wisdom that each person has both masculine and feminine qualities making up their full humanity, the idea of God as in any way feminine might be threatening. However, it is a wisdom we must seek, because it brings psychological and spiritual maturity. Those who are unaware of the historical circumstances of the masculine images of God are liable to stay hidebound to a tradition which is proving increasingly inadequate for our age. To understand God as purely masculine plays into the hands of those who reject Christianity as too patriarchal and who seek to resurrect the ancient goddess in a search for a feminine presence—the very thing which many church people dread.

In a world dominated by the drive for power, exploitation and aggrandisement, not everyone finds images of lordship, kingship and warrior-god or hymns like *Onward Christian Soldiers* helpful. By rejecting the feminine presence and feminine imagery in religion, Christian leaders not only live in the past, but fail tragically to meet the needs of the present. As one minister's wife wrote in the recent Church of Scotland debate,

> At a time when the powerful of the world are so obsessed with doing and having they are losing the art of being; when the world is caught up in the crazy destructive logic of the arms race and the

defence syndrome; when instead of nurturing and
protecting our environment, we are bent on destroying it; never more has the Church and the
world needed those 'feminine' qualities which are
God's gift to mankind, who made it in his own
image.[16]

Despite the obvious wisdom of this position and
indeed its evangelical appeal towards those who are
leaving, or have left, the church because they find it too
masculine, the General Assembly of the Church of
Scotland refused even to discuss the report it had itself
commissioned, dismissing it with curt and grudging
thanks and voting to 'depart from the matter'. The
decision was taken amidst confusion and insult, with
one delegate asking the Woman's Guild president if she
could say whether 'the Divine She who must be obeyed
is a vegetarian or wears a C.N.D. badge!' Reaction had
sunk to such a level. It is ironical, and indeed rather
telling, that the previous day the Assembly had shown
considerable compassion, not to say sympathy, towards
a man who had murdered his mother. This man wanted
to become a Church of Scotland minister and, following
Christ's example, the Assembly acknowledged his
forgiveness and granted permission. The following day
the president of the Woman's Guild was angrily refused
permission to present and discuss a report whose only
crime was that it contemplated the concept of God as
Mother. As an influential group of church people,
including four former Moderators of the General
Assembly, rather wistfully commented: 'It is our belief
that the Church of Scotland is more open, pastoral, and
evangelical than this sad decision suggests.'[17] We may
well ask the question, what are the members of the
Church of Scotland afraid of?

155

iv. *THE ARCHAIC FEAR OF NATURE*

It is likely that subconscious fears of the goddess are also at the heart of the church's disregard for nature, a disregard which, as we have seen, has paved the way for it being in part responsible for the current ecological crisis. Although the church is more guilty of the sin of omission than commission in this, in our present state of crisis all that is necessary for evil to triumph is that we do nothing. The church's indifference to the whole of nature is deplored by many who, like ecologist Lynn White, would define the typically Christian attitude to a tree as 'if you've seen one, you've seen them all'. Fascinatingly, he attributes this indifference to the Christian horror of sacred groves—a horror that pre-dates Christianity, going back to the battle between the Hebrew prophets and the nature religions. 'To a Christian a tree can be no more than a physical fact' he says. 'The whole concept of the sacred grove is alien to Christianity and to the ethos of the West. For nearly two millenia Christian missionaries have been chopping down sacred groves, which are idolatrous because they assume spirit in nature.'[18]

This is what happened to the North American Indians. Tatanga Mani complained that the white men saw them as idolatrous savages because they sang praises to the sun, moon, trees and wind. But they saw the Great Spirit's work in everything, for which they were called pagan. Christians did not so see God's handiwork in his creation; they saw God as the ruler of heaven, and the devil as the ruler of earth.

The Christian propensity to relegate nature to the devil's domain, which rests on a primary reaction to all things 'fleshly', negates the major biblical viewpoint of delighting in it as God's handiwork, a reflection of his glory. (We might recall in passing that the contempt lying behind the epiphet 'pagan' is an extension of the Roman scorn for the low-born, the rustic country-dweller—the *paganus*.) Tatanga Mani protested against the simplistic judgment against his people: 'Indians living close to nature and nature's ruler are not living in darkness.' A return to nature—by a desert or mountain-top experience—was often the only way for God's prophets, (and even his son!) to hear clearly his voice.

The sacredness of nature is by no means alien to the bible itself. According to the priestly ('Elohist') writers, for instance, it was from a burning bush that Yahweh chose to reveal his sacred name to Moses. This was one of the most important moments in the history of God's chosen people, and the fact that God chose a lowly bush from which to declare his name is an indication of how highly he regarded even one of the smallest plants in his creation; he did not destroy it by his presence for 'the bush was burning, yet it was not consumed' (Ex. 3:2). As D M G Stalker points out, 'Fire is a common form in which deity manifests itself. . . . It is the least material of the elements, and when it shoots up, it seems to make a link between earth and heaven'.[19]

Similarly in Jacob's dream at Bethel, while lying in the open air with his head on a stone, '. . . he dreamed that there was a ladder set up on the earth, and the top of it reached to heaven; and behold, the angels of God were ascending and descending on it!' (Gen. 28:12). When he awoke, Jacob exclaimed 'How awesome is this place! This is none other than the house of God, and this is the gate of heaven' (Gen. 28:17). The place he described as the house of God was not a temple, but a field.

Christ's treatment of nature shows that he believed it to be the ready vehicle of God's actions. He told the Pharisees that even if his disciples had not been allowed to praise him as king on his triumphal entry into Jerusalem, the very stones of Jerusalem themselves would have cried out their recognition! The wind which had whipped up the sea while Jesus and his disciples were out in a boat also recognised its lord and became still when rebuked by him. The disciples were amazed that any man could have such power over the elements, and asked 'Who then is this, that even the wind and sea obey him?' Jesus also made constant references to nature's ways in his teaching or examples, comparing the kingdom of heaven to a mustard seed, himself to a mother-hen, and the unanxious life to the existence of the flowers of the field.

When the apostle Stephen was about to be condemned to death by the Jews, having spoken against the temple, his defence was based on the primacy of God in nature over the humanly devised temple. He reminded his persecutors that God preferred his own creation to the temple which his followers so admired. Quoting Isaiah, Stephen told them:

> Heaven is my throne,
> and earth my footstool.
> What house will you build for me, says the Lord,
> or what is my place of rest?
> Did not my hand make all these things?
>
> (Acts 7:49–50)

The bible is full of the glories of creation declaring the handiwork of God:

> The heavens are telling the glory of God;
> and the firmament proclaims his handiwork.
> Day to day pours forth speech,
> and night to night declares knowledge.
> There is no speech, nor are there words;
> their voice is not heard;
> yet their voice goes out through all the earth,
> and their words to the end of the world.
>
> (Ps. 19:1–4)

Yet it is also true that the bible issues stern warnings against worshipping nature herself—the sun, moon, stars and trees, rather than their Creator God. There were, as we have seen, explicit instructions to destroy the sacred and high altars of earlier religions, but this did not mean that the Hebrews could not appreciate the life-force of nature, because this life-force testified to its creator. Christians in general have been so afraid of possible pantheism that they have closed their eyes to the glories of creation. There has been a shying away from too much reverence for nature, calling it 'nature mysticism'. Fear of too close an identification with nature springs from a fear of the goddess's nature religion. This fear of the goddess, now clearly archaic, has been so strong that it has helped create our present ecological crisis. A telling example of 'typically Christian' attitudes can be found in a small World Student Christian Federation book written in 1972 and titled *Ecology and Human Liberation.* Its author, Professor Thomas Derr, while very concerned about the present environmental crisis, nevertheless displayed the kind of sentiments which have helped to cause it. He denied any autonomous value for nature, saying that there is nothing in the bible to establish a value for nature independent of man. He deplored any attempt to personify nature to overcome our sense of separation, and he poured scorn on those 'counter-culture' people who seek an alternative way forward. Although denying that the bible preaches a body-soul dualism in which matter, the body and nature are the source of evil, Derr nevertheless made it clear that in his analysis, nature is only a sort of backdrop to the human drama: 'Nature is a complement to the primary drama of redemption which takes place in history.'[20] God as creator is relegated to the second division; God as redeemer is at the head of the first division. This is precisely the

159

doctrine which Ruether condemns as dualistic. (And in defiance of Paul's asseveration of the *dual* lordship of Jesus—'firstborn of all creation . . . the firstborn from the dead . . .' Col. 1:15–18.) Professor George Hendry points out that when God saw his handiwork in creation he saw that it was good. Good, not only for human beings, but good in itself.[21] The idea that nature is only there for our use has a long tradition, and it is only now being exposed as dangerously mistaken.

A clue to Derr's fear of granting nature any value independent of man can be found in his equally strong resistance to what he called the 'remystifying' of nature. He scorned 'the sentiment . . . that nature's "feelings" are analogous to ours, capable of experiencing human-like offence and pain as the result of our thoughtless cruelty to the natural world',[22] and found it highly significant that some of those who call for a mystical union of humans and nature refer not only to early romantic poetry, but to the Great Mother. According to Derr, it is a sign of romantic poetry's decadence that it very often personifies nature. 'Indeed' he wrote, 'we have today an epidemic of such language, where nature, or the earth, has become "brother", "sister", "she", and the like; even, once in a while, "mother".'[23] Derr was clearly anxious in case the 'remystifying' of nature would in some way resurrect the nature religions and their supreme deity, the Great Mother. He attributed such personifications to alien influences from the east and to counter-culture eccentrics, ignoring or dismissing as irrelevant all personifications of nature. Yet there are many eloquent and moving descriptions of nature in the bible in which we are encouraged and commanded to sense both her elation and her pain. In Chronicles we read how the field and everything in it exults and the trees of the wood sing for joy, (I Chron. 16:33). Isaiah tells how:

the mountains and the hills before you
shall break forth into singing,
and all the trees of the field shall
clap their hands. (Is. 55:12)

In Psalm 114 we are given a most beautiful picture of
the mountains skipping like rams and the hills like
lambs. No doubt the Hebrews could hear the song of
the woodland trees and the dance of the mountains.
How sad it is that so many people have hidden their eyes
and stopped their ears to the exultation of creation.
Again and again the bible poetically personifies creation,
giving it the capacity to experience pain, sorrow and joy.
Paul himself likened creation to a mother groaning and
travailing in childbirth, 'From the beginning till now the
entire creation, as we know has been groaning in one
great act of giving birth' (Rom. 8:22, *Jerusalem Bible*).
It is not simply a trendy counter-cultural whim to
attribute human characteristics to nature, nor is it purely
an eastern concept to imbue nature with the spirit of
God. The Christian tendency to separate spirit from
nature, heaven from earth, God from creation, has
contributed to our modern drive towards exploitation.
The Hebrews had no such split. In the bible creation is
not portrayed as inferior and peripheral—the backdrop
to the human drama. It is God's arena. God spoke
through his creation, and in one sense it was his book as
much as the bible itself. This has been called heresy;
'natural theology' has been all but outlawed by some,
yet as we observed earlier, heresy means to see things
partially, not as a whole. The American Indians saw
another part of the whole but were massacred for it.
'Civilised people depend too much on man-made
printed pages' Tatanga Mani commented. 'I turn to the
Great Spirit's book which is the whole of his creation
. . . the Great Spirit has provided you and me with an

opportunity for study in nature's university, the forests, the rivers, the mountains and the animals which include us.'[24]

God frequently spoke to the Hebrews through nature. They gauged their relationship to their maker by the fertility of the earth, the richness of the harvest, and the regularity of the rains. Yet they failed to recognise the supreme importance of the fertility of the land which God had given them, and failed to keep the sabbatical year which gave it rest and recuperation. It was because of this, as well as their idolatry and injustice to one another, that God caused them to be exiled.

Even so, if we fail to respect the inherent rights of the land to be kept fertile then we too might find ourselves 'exiled'. This is already happening in the places where vital forests are being destroyed and desert lands spreading. So many people in the church refuse these rights to the earth. This attitude to God's creation confirms the accusation that traditional Christianity is one of the most anthropocentric of religions. The very survival of the human race is now endangered by our greed and mismanagement of nature's resources. It may be that for this reason alone enlightened self-interest will motivate attempts to halt the destruction. Nevertheless, the attitude of superiority towards nature, of I'M OK—YOU'RE NOT OK, continues. The fear of granting nature a value of her own, distinct from humanity, is a throwback to the fear of calling her 'mother', of worshipping her seasons, and personifying her cycles: a fear of the goddess.

There was a time, as we have seen, when fear of the power of the goddess was legitimate. There was also a time when fear of the power of nature was legitimate. In the early days nature was mother and she was a goddess. She was not understood; she was a mystery—at times abundant and kind, at times barren and cruel. This was the period of nature religions, which truly personified heaven and the earth, the oceans and the trees. Humankind was at the mercy of the environment, often finding it hostile, destructive and violent. Droughts or floods, earthquakes or volcanic eruptions, pestilences or plagues—so much could destroy the fragile human race. The following Babylonian lament tells of the agony of those suffering drought:

> In Eanna, high and low, there is weeping,
> Wailing for the house of the lord they raise.
> The wailing is for the plants; the first lament is 'they
>   grow not'.
> The wailing is for the barley; the ears grow not.
> For the habitations and flocks it is; they produce
>   not.
> For the perishing wedded ones, for perishing
>   children it is:
> the dark-headed people create not.
> The wailing is for the great river; it brings the flood
>   no more.[25]

To people who lived in very close contact with nature, who read messages in clouds, saw spirits in rivers, heard God's voice in the thunder and lightening; to those whose own cycles and rhythms were totally dependent on nature's cycles and rhythms, disasters such as the above must have had a devastating effect physically and psychologically. The Great Mother Nature would then have been like some merciless, bloodthirsty Gorgon or witch. In terms of TA she was the supremely NOT OK parent. TA tells us that the effect of a NOT OK parent on a child can be depression and listlessness. Extreme effects can be unthinking violence and suicidal tendencies. The same applies to the effects of a NOT OK Mother Nature.

163

In some societies nature has been kind and her ways understood. A happy, ecologically balanced life-style has been found. Such is the case with many indigenous tribes and, until the past few centuries, true even in the west. However, in other societies where the environment has been hostile, there has been too much passive submission to the misfortunes of natural disasters and barrenness of soil, a resigned attitude of WE'RE NOT OK—YOU'RE OK. Religious rituals are often designed to appease a fickle and potentially cruel god or goddess of nature. India today is an example of just such a society, for the people tend to be passively resigned to the lot nature has given them. Climate and soil are hostile to agriculture and there is not enough determination to rise above these limitations and improve land fertility, using initiative and more effective tools. The masculine drive seems to be too weak. Significantly perhaps, the Great Mother Goddess is still very strong in India and is often worshipped as the destructive death dealer Kali.

In the west, the opposite is true. We are very far from being passively resigned to nature's whims. Our drive to survive has been extremely strong and our pride in our 'masculine' ability to transcend nature, to penetrate her mysteries and to subjugate her, has been such that our attitude has become self-righteously violent. We have over-developed our masculine traits, and used them to analyse, control and conquer nature, to bring order out of what we saw as chaos, and to make an apparently submissive mistress out of what others saw as a capricious tyrant. In our patriarchal wisdom we have invented increasingly clever tools with which to exploit natural resources for our own use. But the positive psychic connection with nature, and its spiritual meaning, which characterised the so-called primitive understanding has diminished because of our fear and then our pride. Our schizoid culture exploits, rapes, rejects and murders nature.

The western technologist believes he no longer relies on nature. He rates his own inventions far higher than hers. He believes himself to be the master of nature, free to use her for his needs and then abandon her. He has made himself and his world schizoid because he has convinced his followers that they have no more need of nature, their mother. She has been made into the sort of distant, undemonstrative, uncaring parent, who creates the schizoid problem. Those of her children who have believed the promises of the proud, rebellious and brilliant technocrats have, as Freud and others observed, been made anxious, restless and unhappy, eventually prepared to give vent to their frustration through acts of violence.

We are being warned increasingly often, that the rejection of the wisdom of nature is now so great that we are endangering our lives. We live under the threat of global destruction from that monster of monsters, the nuclear bomb; we risk polluting our earth irreparably for thousands of years through nuclear waste; we spew vast oil-slicks into the sea, bringing cruel death to countless creatures; we tear up our trees, ignorant and regardless of their worth; we tamper with our climate; we create deserts where there were rich lands; we cut ourselves off from the rhythms of nature in high-rise flats, huge cities and treeless streets. We have lost many of the ancient secrets which nature has to offer, and are inexpressibly impoverished as a result. She who was once an oppressor is now our victim; but in polluting her, we pollute ourselves. Our proud, vicious and self-righteous attitude of WE'RE OK—YOU'RE NOT OK, caused by an archaic fear of the uncertainties of nature and the feminine, has led to the certainty of global death, if we do not change direction. The way ahead is not by a return to the goddess, but a realisation of the truly feminine; not by nature-worship, but in a new understanding of God and creation.

Chapter Eight

Freeing the feminine

At the still point of the turning world. Neither flesh
  nor fleshless;
Neither from nor towards; at the still point, there
  the dance is,
But neither arrest nor movement. And do not call it
  fixity,
Where past and future are gathered. Neither
  movement from nor towards,
Neither ascent nor decline. Except for the point,
  the still point,
There would be no dance, and there is only the
  dance.[1]

T S Eliot

There is a rhythm in the cycles of creation which bears
the imprint of its maker, permeating every living thing:
the quiet rise and fall of breath, the pulsations of blood,
the ebb and flow of tide, the revolution of planets, the
cycles of birth, death and rebirth at the heart of the
seasons and of life. Light and dark, activity and
passivity, growth and rest—everything is in a state of
perpetual change and transformation. When we are in
tune with these great rhythms and reflect them in our
lives, then we are on the way to being whole and
creative. But this cosmic dance can only be fully
understood in ourselves and in the world when we are
still, for the still point is at the heart of all things:

> Empty yourself of everything.
> Let the mind rest at peace.
> The ten thousand things rise and fall
> While the Self watches their return.
> They grow and flourish and then return to the
>   source.
> Returning to the source is stillness, which is the
>   way of nature.[2]

Although this may seem highly mystical, perhaps unintelligible to some, it offers a truth which is basic to life. At the heart of the perpetual cycle of opposites there is a core which inspires their movement, which yet transcends it. That core is God. If the much needed union of yin and yang, activity and passivity, masculine and feminine is to be found, then the perception which comes out of creative silence is of vital importance.

Unfortunately, silence and stillness seem almost impossible for us to attain. Over-active, dominated by the need to justify ourselves by what we *do*, we have learned to despise stillness, calling it sloth. Perhaps it is precisely because it is another aspect of the feminine that productive passivity is given so little value. Monica Furlong observes, 'passivity is receptive, containing, fertile and . . . productive. It is the feminine pole of human experience and neither a man nor a woman can be creative without it.'[3] In a world dominated by masculine busyness, the feminine virtue of creative stillness has simply been written off. But we all need times of reflection to find our way, just as much as we need times of activity to give us context, for

> Action and contemplation only become dynamic in so far as each interacts with the other. If action stands for the 'ego' of man, contemplation stands for his unconscious, and both are needed to make up the whole man. The active side of man needs the

168

contemplative side to resolve the deep questions about aims and meanings, and the direction which action ought to take . . . Without contemplation man ceases to feel himself *rooted*, and without roots there can be no stillness, no security, and no growth.[4]

In today's world there is no doubt that stillness, security and creative growth are rare commodities. As Rollo May complained, we have lost touch with our roots, with ourselves, with our cultural heritage and our ancient connection with nature. In despising stillness, which is the way of nature and of God, we have sacrificed our own sense of meaning and relatedness. We are in danger of losing wisdom, true knowledge and the fulness of life. We refuse to grant them equality with information, invention, intellect and endless activity:

> The endless cycle of idea and action,
> Endless invention, endless experiment,
> Brings knowledge of motion, but not of stillness;
> Knowledge of speech, but not of silence;
> Knowledge of words, and ignorance of the Word
> . . .
> Where is the Life we have lost in living?
> Where is the wisdom we have lost in knowledge?
> Where is the knowledge we have lost in informa-
> tion?
> The cycles of Heaven in twenty centuries
> Bring us farther from God and nearer to the Dust.[5]

It is not only our spirits which are stifled by an over-emphasis on the masculine, on intellect and activity. Our actual brains are also damaged by society's bias towards invention, intellect, speech, analysis and data collection. It is a physiological fact that our brains are divided into two hemispheres, each with distinct capabi-

lities. The left side of the brain governs the right side of
the body, including the right hand, and rules all verbal,
logical, linear processes—reading, writing, speaking,
rationalising, etc. It has been called the major hemisphere because its functions are more easily assessed and
are in fact more dominant than those of the right side. It
was only recently that the functions of the right
hemisphere were begun to be understood. It governs the
left side of the body, including the left hand and governs
the intuitive, non-verbal, artistic and holistic qualities. It
has been called the minor hemisphere. We all need both
halves of our brains in order to function as normal
human beings; the more in balance they are, the greater
our personal wholeness. People who suffer brain damage to one side or another can face basic problems as a
result, such as loss of speech or the inability to
remember music. Yet it would appear that it is the left
side of the brain and its functions which historically
have been valued and developed, while the right side has
been considered inferior, and subservient to the left.

This prejudice comes across quite clearly in the
connotations associated with left- and right-handedness.
The right hand, governed by the left side of the brain is
far stronger and more dominant than the left hand. But
it has also been given moral qualities through language,
which imply that its functions are intrinsically better
than those of the left hand. For instance, the word 'right'
means correct, true, proper, just, in English; and in
German and French and other languages the words for
right (*recht* and *droit,* etc.) also mean 'law'. 'Left'
however is 'gauche' in French and 'sinister' in Latin—
whose meaning is clear enough! 'Left-handed' in English
is defined in the *Concise Oxford Dictionary* not only as
awkward and clumsy, but 'ambiguous', double-edged,
of doubtful sincerity or validity . . . ill-omened, sinister.'
These definitions reflect an ancient fear of that part of

the brain which governs the left hand, and thus the intuitive, non-verbal, and imaginative aspects. As Betty Edwards says, '. . . it's important to remember that these terms were all made up, when languages began, by some persons' left hemispheres—the left brain calling the right bad names! And the right brain labelled, pinpointed and buttonholed—was without a language of its own to defend itself.'[6]

There seems almost to have been a plot against the right side of the brain whose functions are remarkably similar to those of the feminine. Indeed, Fritjof Capra has remarked 'The deep-rooted preference for the right side—the one controlled by the left brain—in so many cultures makes one wonder whether it may not be related to the patriarchal value system.'[7] Chinese yin-yang philosophy, numerology, psychology, so many wise systems of knowledge warn against such an imbalance, yet we have proceeded relentlessly with our preference for the collection of facts, frenzied activity and competitiveness rather than intuitive silence, creative stillness and a sense of oneness. Nowhere is this split between the two areas clearer than in the realm of education. Education takes upon itself the training of our minds, yet there is no comparison between the value and attention given to the three 'r's'—functions of the left side of the brain, and art, music and spiritual awareness—functions of the right. Our education is heavily weighted towards the verbal, logical and analytical aspects of life; and against the non-verbal and intuitive. Yet this means that half of our brain is under-developed.

Charles Darwin discovered the dangers of exclusive concentration on the left side of the brain. Until the age of thirty he had a very good balance between both modes of thinking—the intellectual and the artistic. He was very fond of music, art, poetry and literature,

171

especially Shakespeare. However, as he dedicated his life more and more obsessively to scientific research, he found that the right side of his brain had atrophied, and that he had lost his ability to appreciate the gentler arts. To his great dismay, Shakespeare had become 'nauseatingly dull', and music and art increasingly meaningless.

> My mind seems to have become a kind of machine for grinding general laws out of large collections of facts, but why this should have caused the atrophy of that part of the brain alone, on which the higher tastes depend, I cannot conceive. . . . The loss of these tastes is a loss of happiness, and may possibly be injurious to the intellect, and more probably to the moral character by enfeebling the emotional part of our nature.[8]

There is nothing wrong with collecting facts, analysing problems, or strenuous intellectual activity, just as there is nothing wrong with any of the masculine areas of life, *so long as they are held in balance.* Darwin was a victim of his age—an age which deified the 'scientific method'. He felt himself to be in danger of losing his moral perceptions as well as impairing his mind, through the repression of his artistic feelings. His brain had become a sort of fact-finding factory and knowing this made him miserable and deeply anxious. We may well ask ourselves if, in our reductionist technological age, our brains and moral and imaginative sensibilities are not being impaired by our concentration on reason at the expense of intuition, science at the expense of artistic perception, a reduced part at the expense of the whole?

There are many who would dispute this hotly, as did Professor Derr at an ecological conference which Theodore Roszak was addressing.[9] Roszak was trying to put across his theory that the ills of our industrial society

are partly caused by our bias towards rational understanding, verbal expression and analytical dissection of
problems—in other words towards the left side of the
brain, the masculine. He believed that this was imbalanced, forcing us into a narrow constricting box of
rationality from which we must escape in order to learn
how to act spontaneously and enjoy ecstasy and intuitive
feeling, to celebrate life's fulness. In horrified
tones, Derr reported that this was to be at the expense of
education, science and rational thought. With considerable relish he described the counter-attack which came
most notably from a number of economists, a judge and
a molecular biologist. They showed utter contempt for
Roszak's suggestions, poured scorn on his analogies,
and insisted that being men in official capacities, they
wished to remain rational and 'stay in the box'. We can
guess why the aspects of life ruled by the right side of the
brain have been called sinister, and ill-omened: people
have been terrified of losing control and thereby 'losing
face'. The schizoid fear of letting go is very apparent in
Derr's account.

In a fascinating book titled *Drawing on the Right Side
of the Brain*, the American artist Betty Edwards tells
how many people's fear of self-expression through
painting and drawing is due to their inability to trust the
intuitive promptings of their right brain.[10] The dominant verbal cleverness of the left side of the brain has to
be taught to be still and play the subservient role. Only
then can the spatially and artistically talented right side
of the brain get to work. Edwards achieved some
astonishing results from her training classes, where the
artistically inept became accomplished in a matter of
weeks. Clearly, there is still a great deal to be discovered
about the depth and scope of the feminine in us.

Wordsworth knew the value of letting the truth speak
through the non-verbal part of our brain, in the stillness

of repose and meditation. Replying to a friend's criticism of his laziness in day-dreaming instead of reading an improving book, he wrote:

> The eye—it cannot choose but see;
> We cannot bid the ear be still;
> Our bodies feel, wher'er they be,
> Against or with our will.

> Nor less I deem that there are Powers
> Which of themselves our minds impress;
> That we can feed this mind of ours
> In a wise passiveness.

> Think you, 'mid all this mighty sum
> Of things for ever speaking,
> That nothing of itself will come,
> But we must still be seeking?[11]

This 'wise passiveness' with which Wordsworth suggests we feed our minds can bring a richness to our beings, a sense of the wholeness and beauty of our world, and the ability to see into its heart. Meditation is a form of this wise passiveness by which we tune into the stillness of our Creator, and receive a new sense of harmony—and discord—in the universe. In meditation both sides of our brain are used, so it is the whole person who is at one with the Creator. In his perceptive book *Silent Music* William Johnston explores the spirit and science of meditation, comparing eastern and western traditions. There are many similarities between them, but some significant differences. Significantly, many people are looking to the east for new models and inspiration, in their search for wholeness and for relief from scientific reductionism. However, as Johnston points out, a fusion of eastern and western traditions is more helpful to us today, for alone each has its limitations.

The west is a predominantly left-brain culture, and even in meditation and prayer there has been considerable concentration on verbal communication: requests, intercessions, masses, etc. The dualities and conflicts of life are clearly perceived, as our creeds demonstrate, and there is a strong—and masculine!—awareness of our uniqueness of faith, our separate identity from God and the distinctiveness of own personalities. The paradox of the oneness of God and the variety of his creation has given rise to considerable intellectual debate. Johnston aptly remarks, 'From Parmenides and Heraclitus to Plato, and from Aristotle to Thomas Aquinas the words rang out in syllogistic disputations: "How can it be that there is only one thing and yet there are many things? . . ." While eastern philosophy scarcely considered the problem, its Hellenistic counterpart set up two opposing and irreconcilable systems, two opposing camps: monism and dualism, pantheism and monotheism.'[12] It is this perennial perception of conflicting opposites which has helped to create our schizoid mentality, and freeze the feminine.

Japan, by contrast, despite her rapid progress along the technological road, still appears to be a predominantly right-brain culture. Zen Buddhism, for instance, dismisses the rational, intellectual, discriminating mode of thinking as illusory, of no use in the practice of meditation. Zen always reaches towards the holistic and non-discriminating consciousness, where all is one. As Johnston has stated, eastern philosophy scarcely considered the problem of the one and the many; it was simply a non-issue. Many accuse Christianity of over-emphasising its ordinary verbal, intellectual prayers and praise, at the expense of a mystical, spiritual contemplation. The accusation appears to be well-founded. But Zen is equally imbalanced in its total rejection of the rational process—and thus of one side of the brain.

175

These systems need not contradict one another, nor perpetuate the clashing of opposite views. Our schizoid polarisations can be healed if we realise that these states of awareness—the masculine and feminine, the left and right sides of the brain—are equally vital, and complementary to each other. In meditation (or contemplation) Johnston describes three levels of consciousness which are part of a whole, which together give us clear perceptions of the dualities and difficulties of life. Out of this comes the awareness that in the eternal plan such divisions and frictions are of no significance: that all is one in God, and God wills to be at one with us. We might call these the masculine consciousness, the feminine consciousness and the union of the two.

The first, Johnston calls the discriminating rational consciousness. This is what is experienced in normal life, at business, in science and in scholarship. It is also experienced in much Christian worship and meditation. For some this is as far as consciousness goes, but for others it is only the first step on their spiritual path.

The second level is that of the undifferentiated consciousness. This is experienced in Christian mysticism. There is a sense of barriers being broken down, of being absorbed into the womb of creation, of the creator himself, and an awareness of the illusory nature of conflicts. This is the feminine perception, and as Johnston says: 'To the person who experiences this oneness in a momentary intuition, it may become difficult to believe again in duality; just as the person without that experience of unity can only believe in duality.'[13]

The third stage is like a marriage of the two, a 'transforming union' in which there is simultaneous awareness of total unity in the midst of duality. 'This is the experience of the mystic who realises in a flash of ecstatic love that only God exists and that God is the all—and yet, at the same time, that he himself also exists as a unique person, called by name and loved definitively.'[14] This stage can be experienced equally in prayer and at work, as Brother Lawrence had found when he wrote: 'The time of business . . . does not with me differ from the time of prayer; and in the noise and clutter of my kitchen, while several persons are at the same time calling for different things, I possess God in as great tranquillity as if I were upon my knees at the Blessed Sacrament.'[15]

It is fascinating to discover that this third stage is often called 'the mystical marriage'. It is seen as the inner core of our perception of life, the 'holy of holies' of spiritual experience. Analogies are often drawn with the love-imagery of the Song of Songs, which spoke of the marriage of heaven and earth—God at one with his people, spirit united with matter, the masculine forces penetrating the feminine and the feminine responding to the masculine. As in a human marriage the man and woman experience a sense of transcending their separateness in the ecstasy of love while yet maintaining their individuality, the paradox of supreme self-fulfilment in self-giving, so in the mystical marriage, the believer feels totally at one with and absorbed by God—in heaven as it were—while also ever conscious of being an individual with feet planted firmly on earth. It is the marriage of heaven and earth.

This being so, we would expect those who experience this mystical marriage to value the material, daily matters of earth as highly as the spiritual, transcendent experiences of heaven. It does seem to be the case; for instance, at the very consummation of contemplation, the great mystic Theresa of Avila never lost sight of the humanity of God manifested in Christ. It was a point she stressed again and again. This was reflected in her own humanity and in the considerable achievements of her life. She had little respect for any reputedly great spiritual leader who could not face the drudgery of daily chores.

Thomas Merton, that profoundly influential contemporary mystic, was eventually as involved with political and social issues as he was with the inner life. For him too there could be no divorce between heaven and earth. He wrote, 'In His love we possess all things and enjoy fruition of them, finding Him in them all. And thus as we go about the world everything we meet and everything we see and hear and touch, far from defiling, purifies us and plants in us something more of contemplation and of heaven.'[16]

It is a travesty of the true contemplative and spiritual life to see it as separate from the issues of our day. Jesus himself was a rebel. He offered peace, but not at the cost of truth or reality. Kenneth Leech makes this point in his book *The Social God,*

> The Christian pursuit of contemplation does not take place in space, but within this broken and fallen world-order. Contemplation has a context: it does not occur in a vacuum. Today's context is that of the multinational corporations, the arms race, the strong state, the economic crisis, urban decay, the growing racism, and human loneliness. . . . It is in the midst of chaos and crisis that [the contemplative] pursues the vision of God and experiences the conflict which is at the core of the contemplative search. He becomes part of that conflict and begins to see into the heart of things.[17]

Kenneth Leech might well have added the ecological crisis to his list of modern problems. Since an intense love for nature seems to be a common experience among mystics of all traditions, one would expect to find ecologists among the world's most spiritual people. Zen teaches that we start with the awareness that 'I am breathing' and then move to the awareness that 'the universe is breathing'. The sense of the unity of being, experienced in stillness, extends to the whole of creation. If the universe is groaning, then we should be aware of it. John of the Cross saw his beloved God in all of nature. 'My beloved is the mountains, the solitary wooded valleys, strange islands . . . silent music,' he wrote. Presumably if the mountains had been blasted, the solitary wooded valleys chopped down, and the strange islands polluted, then his silent music would have sounded more like a cacophony. Thomas Merton saw animals, flowers, trees, all of nature as worshipping God just by being themselves: 'A tree gives glory to God first of all by being a tree. For in being what God means it to be, it is imitating an idea which is in God and which is not distinct from the essence of God, and therefore a tree imitates God by being a tree.'[18] If those who are cutting down the Brazilian rain-forests at the rate of twenty million hectares a year saw each tree as being part of the imprint of God, would they be able to pursue their massacre?

The Christian mystic who did most to redeem nature from her alienated category of the exploitable other, was Francis of Assisi. He loved the things of nature with an intensity that was almost sensual—'Blessed Francis, wholly wrapped up in the love of God, discerned perfectly the goodness of God not only in his own soul, now adorned with the perfection of virtue, but in every creature.'[19] He sang the praises of the birds, stones, woods and flowers, addressing a hymn of thanksgiving to Brother Sun, Sister Moon, Brother Wind, Sister Water, Brother Fire and Sister Mother Earth. He is famous for addressing his sermons to the birds and for their trust in him. Because of his great humility towards the plant, animal and mineral kingdoms, never showing

179

any manipulative or exploitative attitudes, Francis has appropriately been called the patron saint of ecologists.

One does not have to be a saint however, or even a mystic, to experience the love of God, in turn transporting us to a deep love for all his creation. Today, when we are being continually informed about the tragic state of our environment, the extinction of animals through our greed, and the starvation of millions of fellow human beings, those of us who know and love the Creator-Spirit should feel compelled to enter into the struggle to protect, rescue and restore creation.

The vision and the resources to engage in this struggle are given when we become still before God. Stillness is not the monopoly of mysticism, it is at the very heart of the bible and involves one of its most inviolable laws: 'Be still and know that I am God.' We read that God, the originator and creator of the rhythms of life, worked at his creation for six days and rested on the seventh. He commanded his people to do likewise every seven days, and he commanded them to allow their fields and animals to rest every seventh year. It was part of God's rhythm of withdrawal and return that every seventh day and every seventh year productivity be stopped.

The meaning of sabbath *(shabbat)* is literally desist or stop. As Erich Fromm points out, this stopping is vital for re-establishing harmony and balance in ourselves, in our human relationships, and in our relationship with nature. His interpretation of how we worship God on that day is very similar to Merton's view of a tree worshipping God—we just need to be ourselves. 'It is not rest *per se*, in the sense of not making an effort, physically or mentally,' he writes,

> It is rest in the sense of the re-establishment of complete harmony between human beings and between them and nature. Nothing must be des-

180

troyed and nothing be built: The Shabbat is a day of truce in the human battle with the world. ... . On the Shabbat one lives as if one *has* nothing, pursuing no aim except *being*, that is, expressing one's essential powers: praying, studying, eating, drinking, singing, making love.[20]

Important though it may be to stop and rest even for one day out of seven, many of us find this almost impossible to do. We are so obsessed with getting and spending, having and doing, that we seem to have no time just to be, but this is at tremendous cost to our own wholeness, and potentially very dangerous for society in general. Over-expansion, uncurtailed activity, aggressive competition and blind ambition are dominant features of our world. The wisdom of meditation, the poise of stillness and the creativity of quiescence are dismissed as little more than an excuse for unhealthy introspection and idleness.

In her book, *Contemplating Now*, Monica Furlong recommends that everyone takes an extended period of rest at least once in their lives, but warns that learning how to stop can be a very painful process. Unvoiced fears and disturbing thoughts which have lain dormant while we were active have a tendency to come crowding into our minds like difficult children demanding attention. In these very fears and anxieties, however, lie the seeds of our healing. They are like weeds that spring up in fallow soil, pointing us to deficiencies and needs that we would otherwise miss or try to repress. If we allow ourselves to face the anguish, self-doubt and anxiety of this time, we emerge refreshed and invigorated, with a new vision about ourselves and the beginning of an awareness of what it means to be whole:

We may take weeks to get to this point, weeks in which we struggle with guilt at our 'laziness', and

181

with a growing sense of depression and self-dissatisfaction. If we can persist with this then we reach a sort of nub or core of the experience. Our depression becomes very great, there is a strong sense of pain and darkness, and we find ourselves gazing down into the deep springs of our personalities, and of life itself.

If we can stay with this sense of pain and loss, then we are assured by Monica Furlong that we shall find our way back:

> Once we have reached this still point, and have rested at it, however briefly, then we begin to move, slowly at first, back towards activity . . . and one by one we can again pick up the tasks that interest us, and which seem proper to our development, finding that we see them with new eyes. We have a new vision about ourselves and our lives.[21]

A new vision is certainly what we need today, ruled as we are by archaic fears of the feminine aspects of life. If we do not listen to the promptings of our own instinctual need for rest, renewal and spiritual refreshment, it is not only we who will suffer break-down; the whole of society will begin to crumble.

Monica Furlong tells us that passivity belongs to the feminine pole of human experience and no woman or man can be creative without it. It is very striking that in the west it is the catholic rather than the protestant tradition that values creative passivity, the mystical way of stillness and the power of meditation. The openness to the feminine in this way may well owe something to the influence of Mary. Although her veneration has done nothing to improve the lives and status of actual women themselves—indeed it has done them great

harm—nevertheless her presence in catholic consciousness has had a feminising effect.

In the reformed tradition, by contrast, it is the
masculine work-ethic which still seems to be dominant,
with many people showing great suspicion of silence,
stillness and contemplation. There seems to be a fear that
by tuning in to the breathing of creation and the rhythm
of our own breathing we shall find, not God, but the
devil. In abandoning ourselves to silent prayer we yield
ourselves up to God and find ourselves welcomed into
our begetter's womb. Such a thing is terrifying for those
who have a dread of the feminine and as we have seen,
many Christians do indeed have just such a dread. This
was most strikingly illustrated in the Church of Scotland's debate on the 'Motherhood of God'. Many
thought it was Mary who was being addressed as 'Dear
Mother God' in a prayer at the Annual Meeting of the
Woman's Guild of the Church of Scotland in 1982, and
expressed an almost hysterical horror that such a
'papish' concept could have found its way into the kirk.
However, as the kirk's own study-report on the matter
coolly observed, 'There are those who believe that the
reluctance of a Reformed church to give recognition to
Mary betrays a fear of femininity as much as a fear of
Rome . . .'[22]

Many of those who object to the prominence given to
Mary by the Catholic Church point behind her to the
towering figure of the pagan goddess. Mary did inherit
many of the characteristics of her predecessors and, as
we have seen, is often depicted seated on a throne with
Christ on her lap in a manner reminiscent of Isis; she is
known by Ishtar's name, Queen of Heaven; she is the
virgin-mother, as were many goddesses; and her title
Mother of God is strikingly similar to the Great
Goddess's title Mother of the Gods. However, Mary is
not a goddess, nor technically speaking is she worship-

ped by Rome. She is venerated as the mother of Christ, the first Christian, and an example of how the Christian life should be lived.

Why does her name and that of the Great Goddess arouse such fear? It is almost as if the ancient power of the Great Mother continues as strong as ever, despite the opposition of Judaism and Christianity. Is her religion not dead? Does she really threaten our churches as those who fear calling God 'Mother' appear to believe?

i. *THE RETURN OF THE GODDESS*

In a remarkable book by Edward C Whitmont, a leading Jungian analyst, the following astonishing claim has recently been made:

> At the low point of a cultural development that has led us into the deadlock of scientific materialism, technological destructiveness, religious nihilism, and spiritual impoverishment, a most astounding phenomenon has occurred. A new mythologem is arising in our midst and asks to be integrated into our modern frame of reference. It is the myth of the ancient Goddess who once ruled earth and heaven before the advent of patriarchy and of the patri-archal religions.[23]

This figure has already found her way into even the most conservative Christian churches. What does her appearance signify? Whitmont continues,

> The Goddess is now returning. Denied and suppressed for thousands of years of masculine domination, she comes at a time of dire need. In the depths of the unconscious psyche, the ancient Goddess is arising. She demands recognition and homage. If we refuse to acknowledge her, she may

unleash forces of destruction. If we grant the Goddess her due, she may compassionately guide us toward transformation.[24]

What can this mean? It seems to confirm the very worst fears of those who have a dread of the feminine. Has the nightmare of the goddess returning become a reality? Who is this goddess who demands recognition? Is she a pagan deity resurrected from the past?

The goddess who arises in our midst is not the historical Ishtar-Astarte, nor is she Isis, Gaia or Kali, yet paradoxically she is all of these. The goddess who arises is no threat to almighty God, the transcendent being who made us all and who, although we call him Father, utterly transcends physical and psychological definitions. The goddess who demands acknowledgment is an *archetype,* a model which lives in the unconscious psyche of each one of us and relates to certain ancient forms of human thought and experience. She is as much a part of creation as we are ourselves and her power, which lies in our unconscious minds, is at its strongest when we fear her most.

As we know, nature has from the beginning of time been personified as a goddess, and various religious traditions have worshipped her as protector and sustainer of life. These traditions have left their mark on our 'collective unconscious', that part of our psyche which has a connection with the common historical and psychological heritage of humanity. It was Jung who discovered this aspect of our unconscious, finding that just as there is an evolutionary history behind the human body, so there is also an evolutionary history behind the mind. The immensely old psyche of primitive people forms the basis of our modern minds in the same way as the ancient physical structure of all mammals is akin to our skeletal frame. As Jung explained,

The trained eye of the anatomist or the biologist finds many traces of this pattern in our bodies. The experienced investigator of the mind can similarly see the analogies between the dream pictures of modern man and the products of the primitive mind, its 'collective images', and its mythological motifs.[25]

These collective images which Jung called archetypes arise in our dreams, fantasies, myths; and in the very structures of society itself. Sometimes when a person or group is dealing with some basic life-situation such as giving birth, facing death or overcoming conflict, the experience is perceived through images which are not consciously understood, but relate to the perception of the experience which is the common inheritance of humanity since before rationality. These images are the archetypes and are of such antiquity and complexity that it is almost impossible to describe them, yet it is vital that we gain some insight into their meaning for they exert tremendous power. Jung warned that,

> Archetypes . . . are psychic forces that demand to be taken seriously, and they have a strange way of making sure of their effect. Always they were the bringers of protection and salvation and their violation has as its consequences the 'perils of the soul' known to us from the psychology of primitives. Moreover, they are the infallible causes of neurotic and even psychotic disorders, behaving exactly like neglected or maltreated organs or organic functional systems.[26]

The archetypal Great Mother relates to the early days of human history when nature was mother—both cruel and kind, life-giver and death-dealer. The realm of human experience which she makes us face is that of the

186

suffering, destructive and transformative processes of physical life. She symbolises the great cycles of birth, death and resurrection: cycles which can be found in the seasons, in daily life and in the spiritual mysteries. Hers is 'a wisdom of the unconscious and the instincts of life and relatedness.'[27] She points to the oneness of all life and releases the power of our intuitions, feelings and desires in both their positive and negative guise. She rules both the ecstatic heights of joy and the depths of despair, bringing the threat of dismemberment and death but also the promise of purification and new life.

It is the Great Mother within who forces us to bring our feelings into the open. If we do not obey, then our creativity is stifled and we are unable to love ourselves or others. 'Achieving authenticity necessitates honoring one's emotional needs and desires',[28] says Whitmont. Repression of one's emotions, even those we dislike, is exceedingly dangerous. It is like trying to cover up a sceptic wound. If the infected pus is not in some way expressed it will course through the body, poisoning its systems and creating serious disorders. As ruler of our deepest emotions, darkest desires and most unacceptable feelings, the goddess forces us to acknowledge those aspects of ourselves which we least admire. In historical terms, it was the darker sides of the vegetation rites—the sacred prostitution, orgiastic ceremonies and blood sacrifices which corresponded to this realm of fear, darkness and destruction in ourselves. In this guise she is Kali, the bringer of death, but it is a death that can remove decay and putrefaction and lead on to fresh, healthy growth.

Whitmont explains something of the dual role of the Great Mother by comparing her activities to the dynamics between the female ovum and the male sperm at the moment of conception. It is his belief that anatomy and physiology follow the same archetypal

187

patternings to be found in the psyche. Thus the dynamics between the egg and sperm echo the interplay between the feminine and masculine principles in each person. In the womb the ovum at first passively receives the highly-active sperm, but once the sperm has penetrated her boundaries, the roles are reversed: she becomes the active partner and sets about dissolving and dismembering the sperm cell in order to make possible the creation of the embryo:

> Although outwardly the feminine receives and submits to aggressive penetration, in the inner invisible mystery of her being she actively dissolves and dismembers in order to re-create, whereas the outwardly aggressive male, in this inner sanctuary, experiences the bliss of surrender to a different kind of wisdom.[29]

Just as the male sperm appears to be destroyed, but is in fact being re-created, so the death which the Great Mother brings leads on to transformation and rebirth. She is the crucible, the melting pot, the vessel into which the potential of our darker selves is poured, to be purified and made new. In her role as transformer, the goddess has the power to change the most violent of human urges into their spiritual counterpart. Her message is that both in creation itself and in the spiritual and psychological mysteries there often has to be a death, a dying to the pride of an unrealistic self-image, before new life can emerge. This is a truth which can be seen at work in God's created order and it was this message that was being acted out in many of the ancient vegetation cults, albeit in a crude, bloody and primitive way.

In its highest form it is also fundamental to the teaching of Christ, who said 'He who finds his life will lose it, and he who loses his life for my sake will find it'

(Matt. 10:39). He also compared his own death to the sacrifice of the grain of wheat in a way reminiscent of the vegetation rites; 'Truly, truly, I say to you, unless a grain of wheat falls into the earth and dies, it remains alone; but if it dies, it bears much fruit' (John 12:24).

The vegetation rites of the Great Mother were a primitive enactment of the sacrificial dynamics and need for purification and transformation inherent in nature; they have an archetypal meaning which still has a powerful effect on our psyches. It is no coincidence that the myth of the goddess is re-emerging today at a time when some of humanity's most violent attitudes are in evidence in such tragedies as the cruel, silent death of millions of starving children, the malevolent presence of monstrous nuclear arsenals and the mindless abuse of the earth. Because we reject the feminine in our midst, the goddess has taken on her aggressive, ensnaring role. She has been violated and takes her revenge by making us neurotic and fearful. As Whitmont says, we try to repress rather than integrate sensitively the goddess's realm of birth, death and the moods and intuitions of the feminine, and her consort's realm of desire, joy, aggression and destruction, but this has only created

> a widespread sense of depersonalization, frustration, resentment, hate, incapacity to love and insensitivity to the humaness of others and of the self. Primeval envy, greed and destructive hostility increasingly dominate the scene.[30]

This is the potentially explosive schizoid condition which afflicts us today. The feminine which we reject in ourselves, that 'repressed, subjugated and dreaded "abysmal side of man",' as Rosemary Ruether puts it, is projected in its most negative form on to women, mother nature, 'Mother' God, and those feminine qualities which the world so much needs but which it has been taught to despise. How can we find the transforming role of the feminine, that aspect of the Great Mother that purifies rather than devours?

As we have seen, the archetype of the Great Mother makes us face those sides of ourselves of which we are most ashamed and afraid; those thoughts, terrors and temptations which rise up and demand attention when they are least welcome; that shadow-self which we each keep hidden behind our public persona. Healing only comes when we accept these negative aspects in ourselves, acknowledging their power and seeking their transformation instead of fearing them.

Christ is our example in this. The perfect love which he brings is one in which no fear is permissible. He tells us to love our neighbours as ourselves, thereby insisting that we love ourselves as we are, unafraid to face our inadequacies and imperfections. He loves us not because we are perfect and pure but because we acknowledge that we are not. He is the transcendent reality behind the archetype of the Great Mother and it is by his power that our weakness becomes strength. He is the crucible, the melting pot, into which we are thrown to emerge purified, redeemed and made whole; our hurts, fears, hatred and bitterness overcome by the transforming potency of his love.

Christ is not just an archetype. As both creator of the world, dancing with God in the beginning of time and the first-born of his own creation, Christ is the master-craftsman who designed the archetypes, making them pointers to the principles behind his creation. The miracle of the Christian message is that in Jesus Christ these archetypes were incarnated. As we have seen, Jesus was both *logos* and *sophia*, word and wisdom; both the dying and rising God who gave his life for the people, and the sorrowing Mother whose energies restored her son and the land to health. He incarnated, though he also transcended, the drama of the dying god, the mournful search of the mother and the resurrection in the spring. By adopting not only the flesh, but also the archetypes of his own creation, Christ made his mission plain to all humanity. His was to be the final sacrifice as he took upon himself the sin of the world, falling into the earth and dying like the grain of wheat so that there could be a new birth. His sacrifice was once and for all, as was his resurrection. The drama did not have to be re-enacted every year. It was God's own power which, like the archetypal Mother, raised Christ from the dead, and the transforming and eternally renewing energies of God's Spirit are now in us and in the world.

As we have seen, Christ held together the masculine and feminine forces inherent in his creation. We are more familiar with his masculine role, but he is also the good mother whom we in our schizoid distress long for, yet fear. Unlike the bad mother who seems to despise our love-needs, and our hunger for sight and touch, Christ is the mother who is always there, who does not fail in her love and who knows our needs better than we do ourselves. Unlike our schizoid society which rejects the wisdom of mother nature, Christ so valued his own creation that he became part of it, experiencing all its pain and suffering as well as its joy and beauty. He is love incarnate and the renewing power of that love is in us. As Julian of Norwich said,

> In our Mother Christ we grow. In His mercy He reforms and redeems us, and by virtue of His passion, death and resurrection we are made one with Him. This is how our Mother works mercifully for all his children who are yielding and obedient.

> As truly as God is our Father, so truly also God is
> our Mother . . .

> He reveals this in all things, especially in these
> sweet words: 'It is I.' That is to say, 'It is I, the
> power and goodness of the Fatherhood; it is I the
> wisdom of the Motherhood; it is I, the light and
> grace that is all blessed Love; it is I, the Trinity; it is
> I the Unity. I am the highest good of all manner of
> things. I am the one who makes you love. I am the
> one who makes you long. It is I, the fulfilment of
> all true desires.'[31]

ii. *FINDING THE BALANCE*

The maturity of balance which Christ manifested in his
character, relationships and his very being, which
ancient wisdom explored, which our transcendent
creator gave to humanity whom he made in his own
image, that balance is what we need today.

In our over-masculinised world it is the feminine
principle which must be released before that maturity
can come about. As we have seen, all of us, men
included, have the potential to express both the masculine and feminine principles in ourselves. Until now,
however, the feminine has been almost exclusively
associated with women. For this very reason, because
they have been so long identified with the feminine,
women now have a unique responsibility to campaign
for its freedom; to stand up for the earth's rights in an
age of ecological injustice; to call for more respect for
the intuitive sanity that is deep within each one of us; to
demand that men be moved to tears over the misery of
millions of starving and dispossessed people, and the
agony of our raped earth and raped women; to celebrate
the wisdom of shared authority and shared power; to

point the way to a future where co-operation counts more than competition, peace-making more than war-mongering, and love rather than fear is the motivating force behind politicians, industrialists, and priests alike.[32] Women have this special responsibility, not because they are in fact more feminine than men, although many are; not because they are more virtuous, wise, emotional, caring or spiritual; nor because they are closer to nature. They have this responsibility because they have been so exclusively associated with the feminine for so long. It is just as sexist and divisive to attribute all the feminine virtues to woman's nature as it is to attribute all the masculine ones to man's nature. We each possess our own individual mix of both qualities, masculine and feminine. Some people, women included, need to find more of the feminine in themselves; others, men included, need more of the masculine. Neither quality can fulfil its potential in us until we have also accepted, understood, and absorbed its opposite. Wholeness will only be achieved through a new balance of 'opposites'.

There are some women who believe that a return to a matriarchal, rather than a patriarchal, rule is the answer to the world's problems. According to them men have been so spiritually blind and emotionally immature that they can no longer be entrusted with the government of our planet and people. All the main religions are dismissed because, like Christianity, with its traditionally masculine Trinity, they are seen as tainted with patriarchal prejudice. Some of these women are trying to resurrect the ancient goddess religion, in an attempt to release the outlawed feminine. Others turn the accusations of Aristotle, Aquinas, Freud and other detractors of female dignity, back on themselves, calling men morally, spiritually, intellectually, and emotionally inferior to women.

It is understandable that many women are so hurt and angered by their exclusion from a normal humanity, and by the demeaning they have received at the hands of men, that they despise all men and set up barricades against the masculine in any form, calling it evil. But neither is this a mature position, and will not lead us all to wholeness. It is a position of great distress, the TA life position of I'M OK—YOU'RE NOT OK. The answer is not to go out like the criminal psychopath, destroying in bitterness and self-righteousness. The ancients gave clear warning that the feminine must not be allowed to dominate any more than the masculine. Domination by 1080 leads to the rising torrents of a flood. Death comes just as surely from drowning as it does from burning.

Jung warned of the danger of shutting out the psychic opposite, whether animus or anima. We have seen how the churches have rejected the feminine from their midst, for which they are paying the price. They have become possessed by a negative anima which reduces their political credibility, keeps them in a state of retarded growth and too often makes their priests, ministers, committees and official bodies petty, ineffectual and lacking in both courage and initiative. In the same way, those women who reject their own masculinity become possessed by that very masculine in a negative way—the negative animus. So they become cold, critical, self-righteous, insensitive and over-cerebral. It is the positive feminine and the positive masculine qualities which each of us needs in order to be creative. If we could free ourselves of archaic prejudices against either, we might begin to find that maturity of balance which we need in order to grow up whole.

To find that balance we must learn how to be still in the presence of God, where conflict is transcended. This stillness is found at the feminine pole, just as a developing child starts in the primordial silence of the

mother's womb where all is one and at peace. We then
move on to encounter the divisive conflicts and tensions
of identity and separation. This is the masculine force
within us and is vital for the individual's emerging
self-awareness and growth. As Sukie Colegrave says,

> Individually this epoch of the masculine manifests,
> in both sexes, as a time of soaring upwards and
> away from earth, mother, family, instinct and
> nature; a time of separating from the whole, of
> acquiring an individual identity and an ego con-
> sciousness capable of resisting the powerful nostal-
> gic longings to relax into the unconscious. It is a
> time of heroic struggle and achievement; a time of
> setting and pursuing goals; a time of conquest and
> exploration.[33]

Without this masculine energy we do not know the
limits of our capabilities, we do not stretch ourselves
beyond the frontiers of conformity and family taboos,
we do not know ourselves well enough to love
ourselves. However, the masculine in us must yield in
time to the quiescent strength of the feminine which
allows others to come to birth, is not self seeking or
egotistic, does not analyse and reduce but synthesises
and makes whole. If this does not happen, then the
separation from the earth, mother, family instinct and
nature may turn into alienation from these. The ability
to resist the unconscious and find an ego-consciousness
can turn into contempt for the unconscious and over-
emphasis on the superficial egotistic self-conscious
drive; the proving of our strength in heroic struggle,
conquest and achievement can turn into proving our
ability to discover increasingly clever ways of destroying
each other.

We have discovered our technological capacity for
destruction through the unbridled dominance of mascu-

line qualities. This has made us anxious, restless, and insecure. Now, to survive, we must put aside our adolescent desire to prove our independence from nature, and grow up into respectful and reverential relationships with her, with women who have for so long represented her, and with all the feminine qualities that our world so much needs. To rise to this challenge, we must all begin with ourselves, where we are. Having been identified with the feminine weaknesses for so long, women must summon their feminine *and* masculine strengths to rescue the feminine for both men and women. There *is* hope and promise:

> There is a woman who is tired of acting weak when she knows she is strong,
>
> and there is a man who is tired of appearing strong when he feels vulnerable.
>
> There is a woman who is tired of acting dumb, and there is a man who is burdened with the constant expectation of knowing everything.
>
> There is a woman who is tired of being called 'an emotional female' and there is a man who is denied the right to weep and to be gentle.
>
> There is a woman who is called unfeminine when she competes and there is a man for whom competition is the only way to prove his masculinity.
>
> There is a woman who is tired of being a sex object and there is a man who must worry about his own potency.
>
> There is a woman who feels 'tied down' by her children and there is a man who is denied the full pleasure of shared parenthood.

There is a woman who is denied meaningful
  employment or equal pay and there is a man
  who must bear full financial responsibility
  for another human being.

Bringing the promise of *new community:*

There is a woman who takes a step towards her own
  liberation and there is a man who finds the
  way to freedom is made a little easier.[34]

This is only the first step. Once we have found the
balance of the masculine spirit and the feminine spirit in
our souls and psyches, we must go further and seek that
balance in the world about us. When Jesus said, 'You
must be perfect, as your Heavenly Father is perfect', the
word he used means 'complete'. We are commanded to
be complete, whole, as our creator is whole. This completeness does not stagnate; it does not rest in its own
perfection; it cannot be contained in each person,
unused and unchanged. Like the grain of mustard seed
which contains the germ of the masculine and feminine
forces inside its shell, our completeness cannot fail to
burst into new growth. Eventually, with our roots
planted deep in the earth and our branches stretched up
in salutation to heaven, we shall become like the
fully-grown mustard tree, a symbol of the kingdom of
heaven, and find ourselves giving nourishment and
protection to all God's creation.

NOTES TO CHAPTER ONE

1. Sigmund Freud: *Civilization and its Discontents,* translated by Joan Riviere, Hogarth Press, London, 1930, p 144.
2. See Jonathan Schell: *The Fate of the Earth,* Picador, London, 1982.
3. *Ibid.* p 230.
4. *North-South: A Programme for Survival,* introduced by Willy Brandt, Pan, London, 1983.
5. *Ibid.* p 17.
6. *Ibid.* p 16.
7. Anthony Storr: *Human Aggression,* Penguin, 1968, pp 82–89.
8. Rollo May: *Love and Will,* Fountain Books, Glasgow, 1977, p 16.
9. Frank Lake: *Clinical Pastoral Care in Schizoid Personality Reactions,* Clinical Theology Association, 'Lingdale', Western Avenue, Mount Hooton Road, Nottingham, 1971, p 30.
10. *Op. cit.* p 20.
11. *Ibid.* pp 16–17.
12. *Op. cit.* p 27.
13. *Ibid.*
14. J. B. Watson: *Psychological Care of the Infant and Child,* cited by Christina Hardyment: *Dream Babies,* Jonathan Cape, London, 1983, p 175.
15. Rollo May: *Man's Search for Himself,* Allen & Unwin, Ltd., 1953, p 24.
16. May: *Love and Will,* p 14.
17. See Elaine Morgan: *Falling Apart: The Rise and Decline of Urban Civilization,* Abacus, London, 1978, p 14.
18. *Op. cit.* p 42.
19. William Cobbett: *Rural Rides,* cited by Raymond Williams: *The Country and the City,* Chatto and Windus, London, 1973, p 146.
20. William Wordsworth: *The Prelude,* Book VII lines 116–118.
21. *Ibid.* first edition, lines 624–634.
22. Cited by Williams, *op. cit.* pp 215–216.
23. Wordsworth: *Tintern Abbey,* lines 107–111.
24. A. C. Swinburne: *Atalanta in Calydon* (1863–4), cited by Mario Praz: *The Romantic Agony,* Oxford University Press, London, 1970, p. 233.
25. E. F. Schumacher: *Small is Beautiful,* Abacus, London, 1974, p 122.

26. See *The Times,* Thursday June 3, 1980, a Special Report for World Environment Day, entitled *Survival.*
27. Robert Allen: *How to Save the World: Strategy for World Conservation,* Kogan Page Ltd., London, 1980, p 11.
28. Cited in *Touch the Earth, A Self-Portrait of Indian Existence,* compiled by T. C. McLuhan, Abacus, London, 1978, p 56.
29. Kit Pedler: *The Quest for Gaia: A Book of Changes,* Souvenir Press, London, 1979, p 12.
30. *Ibid.* p 11.
31. *Ibid.*
32. C. G. Jung: *Man and His Symbols:* Picador, London, 1978, p 85.
33. *Ibid.* For a full and comprehensive explanation of the archetype of the Great Mother, see Erich Neumann: *The Great Mother, an analysis of the archetype,* Routledge and Kegan Paul, London, 1955.
34. *Op. cit.* p 19.

NOTES TO CHAPTER TWO

1. Lao-tse: *Tao Te Ching,* in *The Wisdom of Laotse,* translated by Lin Yutang, Michael Joseph, London, 1958, p 14.
2. Apuleius: *The Golden Ass,* translated by Robert Graves, Folio Society, 1960, p 190.
3. Mircea Eliade: *From Primitives to Zen,* Collins, London, 1967, p 14.
4. Robert Graves: *Greek Myths,* Cassell, 1958, p 31.
5. Eliade: *op. cit.* p 24.
6. *Ibid.* p 94.
7. Cited by M. Esther Harding: *Woman's Mysteries,* Rider and Co., London, 1971, p 167.
8. S. Langdon: *Tammuz and Ishtar,* Clarendon Press, Oxford, 1914, p vi.
9. *Ibid.* p 1.
10. John Bright: *A History of Israel,* SCM Press Ltd., London, 1982, p 119.
11. Apuleius, *op. cit.* p 190.
12. *Ibid.*
13. E. O. James: *The Ancient Gods,* Weidenfeld and Nicholson, London, 1960, p 85.
14. James: *The Cult of the Mother-Goddess,* Thames and Hudson, London, 1959, p 61.

15. Rosemary Radford Ruether: *Mary—The Feminine Face of the Church*, SCM Press Ltd., London, 1979, p 14.
16. James: *The Cult of the Mother-Goddess*, p 245.
17. See E. S. Hartland: *Primitive Paternity*, David Nutt, London, 1909, and P. Malinowski: *The Father in Primitive Psychology*, Kegan Paul, Trench, Trubner and Co. Ltd., London, 1927.
18. James: *Man and His Gods*, edited by Geoffrey Parrinder, Hamlyn, London, 1973, p 33.
19. For detailed discussion on the historical relationship between matriarchy and patriarchy see J. J. Bachofen: *Myth, Religion and Mother Right*, translated by Ralph Mannheim, Princeton University Press, Princeton 1967; Robert Briffault: *The Mothers*, George Allen and Unwin, London, 1927 and Evelyn Reed: *Woman's Evolution*, Pathfinder Press Inc., New York, 1975.
20. *The Creation Epic*, Tablet IV, lines 83–84, translated by E. A. Speiser: *Ancient Near Eastern Texts Relating to the Old Testament*, ed. James B. Pritchard, Princeton University Press, Princeton, 1955, p 67.
21. *Ibid.* lines 93–104.
22. *Ibid.* lines 138–140.
23. James: *The Ancient Gods*, p 77.
24. Langdon, *op. cit.* p 110.
25. *Ibid.* p 29.
26. James: *Man and His Gods*, p 33.
27. See Langdon, *op. cit.* chs 1/2 and M. Esther Harding *op. cit.* p 98/ch 12 for the dates of Ishtar.
28. See Donald Wiseman: *Man and His Gods*, p 100.
29. Langdon, *op. cit.* p 19.
30. *Hymn to Ishtar* lines 27–32, translated by Ferris J. Stephens: *Ancient Near Eastern Texts*, p 383.
31. *Prayer of Lamentation to Ishtar*, *op. cit.*, lines 1–8; 18–20; 39–45; 62–78.
32. *Ibid.* lines 79–81; 93–94.
33. *Ibid.* lines 99–105.

NOTES TO CHAPTER THREE

1. Rosemary R. Ruether: *Mary—The Feminine Face of the Church*, SCM Press Ltd., London, 1979, p 15.
2. For detailed descriptions of the snake-goddesses see Merlin Stone: *The Paradise Papers*, Virago, London, 1977, ch 10; S.

Langdon: *Tammuz and Ishtar,* Clarendon Press, Oxford, 1914, ch 3; Esther Harding: *Woman's Mysteries,* Rider and Co., London, 1971, pp 52–54.

3. Georges Contenau: *Everyday Life in Babylon and Assyria,* Edward Arnold Ltd., London, 1954, p 257.
4. S. H. Hooke's commentary on Genesis in *Peake's Commentary on the Bible,* Thomas Nelson and Sons Ltd., Edinburgh, 1962, p 179 para 145c.
5. *Ibid.* p 180 para 147b.
6. *Ibid.*
7. See Merlin Stone, *op. cit.* ch 10 for a fascinating reassessment of the story of Adam and Eve.
8. Gerhard von Rad; *Genesis,* Old Testament Library, SCM Press, London, 1956, p 93.
9. John C. L. Gibson: *The Daily Study Bible: Genesis,* The Saint Andrew Press, Edinburgh, 1981, p 125.
10. Sukie Colegrave: *Sacred Dance, Resurgence* Magazine, May-June, 1981, No 86, p 17.
11. E. O. James: *The Worship of the Sky God,* The Athlone Press, London, 1963, p 30.
12. Walther Eichrodt: *Theology of the Old Testament,* volume one, Old Testament Library, SCM Press, London, 1960, p 186.
13. Emil Brunner: *Man in Revolt,* Lutterworth Press, London, 1953, p 346.

NOTES TO CHAPTER FOUR

1. Wang Ch'ung, cited by Fritjof Capra: *The Tao of Physics,* Fontana, 1976, p 112.
2. *The Oracle of Change,* translated by Alfred Douglas, Penguin, 1977, hexagram one. For a more detailed commentary on all the texts, see the Richard Wilhelm translation: *I Ching,* Routledge and Kegan Paul, London, 1983.
3. *Ibid.* hexagram two.
4. *Ibid.* hexagram one.
5. J. C. Cooper: *An Illustrated Encyclopaedia of Traditional Symbols,* Thames and Hudson, London, 1978, p 196.
6. John Michell: *City of Revelation,* Abacus, London, 1973, p 138.
7. Richard Snead: 'Music and the Mysteries', Spirals, no 13, PO Box 27472, San Francisco, California, 94129.
8. John Michell, *op. cit.* p 140.
9. Cited by John Michell: *The Earth Spirit,* Thames and Hudson, London, 1975, p 4.

10. Cited by Betty Roszak: *The Book of the New Alchemists*, E. P. Dutton, New York, 1977, p viii. See also June Singer: *Androgyny: Towards a New Theory of Sexuality*, Routledge and Kegan Paul, London, 1977, chapter twelve on the inner meaning of alchemy.

11. See June Singer, *op. cit.* on the Tantric tradition.

12. Lao-tse: *Tao Te ching*, number one, translated by Gia-Fu Feng and Jane English, Wildwood House Ltd., London, 1973.

13. C. G. Jung: *Mysterium Coniunctionis: an Inquiry into the Separation and Synthesis of Psychic Opposites in Alchemy*, Routledge and Kegan Paul, London, 1963.

14. C. G. Jung: *Two Essays in Analytical Psychology*, Bailière, Tindall and Cox, London, 1923, p 230.

15. June Singer: *op. cit.* p 50. For a feminist critique of psychoanalysis see also Juliet Mitchell: *Psychoanalysis and Femininism*, Penguin, Harmondsworth, 1974 and Louise Eichenbaum and Susie Orbach: *Outside In . . . Inside Out*, Pelican Books, 1982.

16. Singer, *op. cit.* p 50.

17. *The Motherhood of God:* A Report by a Study Group appointed by the Woman's Guild and The Panel on Doctrine on the invitation of the General Assembly of the Church of Scotland, edited by Alan E. Lewis, The Saint Andrew Press, Edinburgh, 1984, p 19. One of the seminal feminist works on the concept of God is by Mary Daly: *Beyond God the Father: Toward a Philosophy of Women's Liberation*, Beacon Press, Boston, 1973. See also *Motherhood and God*, by Margaret Hebblethwaite, G. Chapman, 1984, for a personal view of God as Mother.

18. *The Motherhood of God*, p 36.

19. *Ibid.* p 66.

20. Jeremiah ch 44, verses 18 and 23.

21. J. C. Cooper, *op. cit.* p 170.

22. J. C. Cooper, *op. cit.* p 45

23 Rudolf Steiner: *Christianity and Occult Mysteries of Antiquity*, translated by E. A. Frommer, Gabrielle Heff and Peter Kändler, Steinerbooks, New York, p 187.

24. *Ibid.* p 193.

NOTES TO CHAPTER FIVE

1. C. Lévi-Strauss: *Les Structures élémentaires de la parenté*, cited by Simone de Beauvoir, *The Second Sex*, Penguin, Harmondsworth, 1981, p 17.

2. Simone de Beauvoir, *Ibid.* p 16.
3. Rosemary R. Ruether: *New Woman; New Earth*, Dove Communications, Victoria, 1975, for a brilliant study of the relationship between sexism, racism and capitalism.
4. Cited by H. R. Hays: *The Dangerous Sex: the myth of feminine evil*, Methuen and Co. Ltd., London, 1966, p 12.
5. Cited by Sukie Colgrave: *The Spirit of the Valley*, Virago, London, 1979, p 76.
6. For a disturbing and angry account of women's sufferings, see *Gyn/Ecology* by Mary Daly, The Women's Press Ltd., London, 1979.
7. See Susan Griffin: *Pornography and Silence*, Women's Press, 1981.
8. *The Scottish Plan of Action for the Decade of Women*, compiled and edited by Cassandra McGrogan and published by the Scottish Joint Action Group, p 22.
9. H. R. Hays, *op. cit.* p 180.
10. Susan Griffin: *Women and Nature, The Roaring Inside Her*, Harper Colophon Books, New York, 1978, pp 52–54.
11. Simone de Beauvoir, *op. cit.* p 105.
12. See *Alice through the Microscope: the power of science over women's lives*, by the Brighton Women and Science Group, Virago, London, 1980.
13. Freud: *Civilization and its Discontents*, translated by Joan Riviere, Hogarth Press, London, 1930, p 73.
14. Carolyn Merchant: *The Death of Nature*, Wildwood House, London, 1982, p xv.
15. Fritjof Capra: *The Turning Point: Science, Society and the Rising Culture*, Wildwood House, London, 1982, pp 21–22.
16. Fritjof Capra: Schumacher Lecture 1979 printed in *Resurgence* Magazine no 78, January-February 1980, p 14.
17. John Michell: *City of Revelation*, Abacus, London, 1973, p 138.
18. Fritjof Capra: *op. cit.* p 24.
19. Lynn White: *The Historic Roots of our Ecologic Crisis*, Science Magazine, March 10, 1967.
20. George S. Hendry: *Theology of Nature*, The Westminster Press, Philadelphia, 1980, p 18.
21. Rosemary Radford Ruether: *Male Clericalism and the Dread of Women*, Student Christian Movement pamphlet, edited by Mary Condren, number 24, p 16.

NOTES TO CHAPTER SIX

1. Tertullian: *De Cultu Feminarum,* I, 1, in Migne, Patrologia Latina (Paris 1944), cited by O'Falain and Martines: *Not in God's Image,* Virago, 1979, p 145.
2. *Luther's Table Talk,* Longman, Rees, Orme, Brown and Green, London, 1832, p 281.
3. Plato: *The Republic,* Book V, 455, translated by D. Lee, Penguin Classics, p 234.
4. Plato: *Timaeus,* edited and translated by J. Warrington, Everyman, London, 1965, 42: B, p 39.
5. Plato: *Laws* Book VI, 781, translated and edited by A. E. Taylor, Everyman, London, 1960, p 164.
6. Aristotle: *Generation of Animals,* translated by A. L. Peck, William Heinemann Ltd., London, 1943, 728a.17, p 103; 775.15, p 461.
7. Thomas Aquinas: *Summa Theologica,* translated by the Fathers of the English Dominican Province, revised by Sullivan, Encyclopaedia Brittanica, Chicago, 1952, Part I, Q 92, Article 1.
8. *Ibid.* Article 2.
9. Erich Neumann: *The Great Mother, an analysis of the archetype,* Routledge & Kegan Paul, London, 1955, p 50.
10. Augustine: *The Works of Aurelius Augustine; On the Trinity,* edited by Marcus Dods, T and T Clark, Edinburgh, 1873, Book XII, chapter VII, pp 291–2.
11. *Ibid.* p 292.
12. *Corpus Iuris Canonici,* edited by A. Friedberg, Leipzig, 1879–81, cited by O'Faolain and Martines, *op. cit.* p 143.
13. Plutarch: *Dialogue on Love* from the French translation by Robert Flacalière, Societé d'Edition les Belles Lettres, Paris, 1952, p 44 ff, cited by O'Faolain and Martines *op. cit.* p 50.
14. Cited by O'Faolain and Martines, *op. cit.* p 11.
15. Tertullian: *Treatises on Marriage and Remarriage, To His Wife,* translated by William P. le Saint, Ancient Christian Writers, volume XIII, Longmans, Green and Co., London, 1951, p 14.
16. Jerome: *The Letters of Jerome,* translated by C. C. Mierow, Ancient Christian Writers, volume XXXIII, Longmans, Green and Co., London, 1963, Letter 22, p 152.
17. Augustine: *The Lord's Sermon on the Mount,* translated by J. J. Jepson, Ancient Christian Writers, volume V, Longmans, Green and Co., London, 1948, p 51.
18. Cited by E. C. McLauglin: *Religion and Sexism,* Simon and Schuster, New York, 1974, p 243.

19. Luther, *op. cit.* p 282.

20. Luther: *Commentary on Genesis: The Creation*, translated by Henry Cole, T and T Clark, Edinburgh, 1858, Chapter III, v 16, p 271.

21. John Knox: *First Blast of the Trumpet against the Monstrous Regiment of Women*, edited by E. Arbor, English Scholar's Library of Old and Modern Classics, London, 1880, p 14.

22. Knox, *op. cit.* p 11.

23. John Calvin in a letter to Sir William Cecil, 1560, cited by Arbor, *op. cit.* p xvi.

24. Karl Barth: *Church Dogmatics; The Doctrine of Creation*, T and T Clark, Edinburgh, 1961, 111/4/172n.

25. *Ibid.* 111/4/171.

26. See *Religion and Sexism, op. cit.* edited by Rosemary R. Ruether, for an excellent over-view of religious attitudes to women in the Jewish and Christian traditions.

27. E. C. McLaughlin, *Ibid.* p 254.

28. Kramer and Sprenger: *Malleus Maleficarum*, translated by M. Summers, The Pushkin Press, London, 1948, Part 1, Question VI, pp 41–47.

29. Summers: *op. cit.* p xiv and xvi.

30. H. R. Trevor-Roper: *The European Witch-Craze of the 16th and 17th Centuries*, Pelican, 1969, p 114.

31. *The Times*, 23 May 1973, quotes the Bishop of Exeter in an article entitled 'Priestesses, "a Shift to Pagan Creeds".'

32. Rosemary R. Ruether: *Male Clericalism and the Dread of Women*, Student Christian Movement pamphlet number 24, edited by Mary Condren, p 16. For further insight into the position of women in the Christian church, see Sara Maitland: *A Map of the New Country: Women and Christianity*, Routledge and Kegan Paul, London, 1983; Susan Dowell and Linda Hurcombe: *Dispossessed Daughters of Eve*, SCM Press, London, 1981, and Margaret and Rupert Davies: *Circles of Community*, published by the British Council of Churches, 1982.

33. George S. Hendry: *Theology of Nature*, The Westminster Press, Philadelphia, 1980, p 117.

34. Rosemary R. Ruether: *Religion and Sexism*, p 152.

35. Frank Lake: *Clinical Pastoral Care in Schizoid Personality Reactions*, Clinical Theology Association, 'Lingdale', Western Avenue, Mount Hooton Road, Nottingham, 1971, introduction.

NOTES TO CHAPTER SEVEN

1. Thomas A. Harris: *I'M OK—YOU'RE OK,* Pan Books, London, 1974, p xvii.
2. *Ibid.* p 217.
3. *Ibid.* p 222.
4. Rosemary Radford Ruether: *Mary, The Feminine Face of the Church,* SCM Press, London, 1979, p 15.
5. Robert Graves: *The White Goddess,* Faber and Faber, London, 1977, p 220.
6. *Ibid.* p 315.
7. J.-J. von Allmen (ed): *Vocabulary of the Bible,* Lutterworth Press, London, 1958, p 146.
8. C. S. Lewis: *Undeceptions,* Geoffrey Bles, London, 1971, pp 191–196.
9. Julian of Norwich: *Revelations of Divine Love,* extracts translated for *Masters of Prayer* Series, the General Synod Board of Education, London, 1984.
10. *The Evening Times,* Thursday, 26 April, 1984, Charles Graham column.
11. *The Scotsman,* Thursday, 27 May, 1982.
12. *The Sunday Mail,* 29 April, 1984, Bernard Falk column.
13. *The Scotsman,* 26 April, 1984.
14. W. A. Visser 't Hooft: *The Fatherhood of God in an Age of Emancipation,* World Council of Churches, Geneva, 1982, p 131.
15. *The Scotsman,* 24 May, 1982.
16. *Ibid.* 31 May, 1982.
17. Published in *Life and Work,* July 1984.
18. Lynn White: 'The Historical Roots of our Ecologic Crisis', *Science* Magazine, 10 March, 1967.
19. D. M. G. Stalker's commentary on Exodus in *Peake's Commentary on the Bible,* Thomas Nelson and Sons Ltd., Edinburgh, 1962, 178c, p 212.
20. Thomas Sieger Derr: *Ecology and Human Liberation: A Theological Critique of the Use and Abuse of our Birthright,* World Student Christian Federation, Geneva, vol III, no 1, 1973, Serial Number 7, p 13.
21. George S. Hendry: *Theology of Nature,* The Westminster Press, Philadelphia, 1980, p 17.
22. Derr, *op. cit.* p 30.
23. *Ibid.*

24. Tatanga Mani, cited by T. C. McLuhan: *Touch the Earth*, Abacus, London, 1973, p 106.
25. Translated by S. Langdon, *Tammuz and Ishtar*, Clarendon Press, Oxford, 1914, p 11.

NOTES TO CHAPTER EIGHT

1. T. S. Eliot: *Four Quartets: Burnt Norton, Collected Poems*, 1902–1962, Faber and Faber, London, 1974.
2. Lao-tse: *Tao Te Ching*, translated by Gia-Fu Feng and Jane English, Wildwood House Ltd., London, 1977, number 16.
3. Monica Furlong: *Contemplating Now*, Hodder and Stoughton, London, 1973, p 21.
4 *Ibid.* p 108.
5. T. S. Eliot: *Choruses from 'The Rock'*, *op. cit.*
6. Betty Edwards: *Drawing on the Right Side of the Brain*, Souvenir Press, London, 1982, p 34.
7. Fritjof Capra: *The Turning Point: Science, Society and the Rising Culture*, Wildwood House Ltd., London, 1982, p 319.
8. Charles Darwin: *Autobiography*, edited by Nora Barlow, William Collins, Sons and Co. Ltd., London, 1958, p 139.
9. For an account see Derr, *Ecology and Human Liberation*, World Student Christian Federation, Geneva, vol 111, no. 1, 1973, Serial Number 7.
10. Edwards, *op. cit.*
11. Wordsworth: *Expostulation and Reply*, Wordsworth Poetical Works, edited by Thomas Hutchinson, Oxford University Press, London, 1969.
12. William Johnston: *Silent Music*, Fontana, Glasgow, 1976, p 82.
13. *Ibid.* p 83.
14. *Ibid.*
15. Brother Lawrence: *The Practice of the Presence of God*, The Epworth Press, London, fourth conversation, p 23.
16. Thomas Merton: *Seeds of Contemplation*, Burns and Oates, London, 1957, p 8.
17. Kenneth Leech: *The Social God*, Sheldon Press, London, 1981, p 53.
18. Merton, *op. cit.* p 9.
19. *St. Bonaventure's Life of St. Francis: The Little Flowers of St. Francis*, Everyman, London, 1966, p 289.
20. Erich Fromm: *To Have or to Be?*, Abacus, London, 1979, p 57.
21. Furlong, *op. cit.* p 115.

22. *The Motherhood of God,* edited by Alan E. Lewis, The Saint Andrew Press, Edinburgh, 1984, p 59.
23. Edward C. Whitmont: *Return of the Goddess,* Routledge and Kegan Paul, London, 1983, p vii.
24. *Ibid.* p viii.
25. C. G. Jung: *Man and His Symbols,* Picador, London, 1978, p 57.
26. Jung: *Essays on a Science of Mythology, Collected Works,* Vol. IX, p 105 cited by Whitmont, *op. cit.* p 28.
27. Erich Neumann: *The Child: Structure and Dynamics of the Nascent Personality,* Hodder and Stoughton, London, 1973, p 53. See also by the same author: *The Great Mother,* an analysis of the archetype, Routledge and Kegan Paul, London, 1955.
28. Whitmont, *op. cit.* p 11.
29. *Ibid.* p 137.
30. *Ibid.* p 12.
31. Julian of Norwich: *Revelations of Divine Love,* extracts translated for *Masters of Prayer* Series, The General Synod Board of Education, London, 1984, p 32.
32. For positive celebrations of the contribution of women see: *Womanspirit Rising,* Harper and Row, New York, 1979; *Walking on Water: Women's Spirituality* by Jo Garcia and Sara Maitland, Virago, 1983, and *Reclaim the Earth: Women Speak Out for Life on Earth* edited by Leonie Caldecott and Stephanie Leland, Women's Press, 1983.
33. Sukie Colgrave: 'Sacred Dance', *Resurgence* Magazine, no 86, p 17.
34. From the *World Council of Churches Consultation on the Community of Women and Men in Church and Society,* Sheffield, 1981, cited by Jack W. Dyce and Ros Lyle in the Congregational Union of Scotland's Assembly White Paper, 1982.

R